Current Approaches to the Prediction of Violence

Progress in Psychiatry

David Spiegel, M.D.,
Series Editor

Current Approaches to the Prediction of Violence

Edited by
David A. Brizer, M.D.
Martha Crowner, M.D.

American Psychiatric Press, Inc.

1400 K Street, N.W.
Washington, DC 20005

Note: The authors have worked to ensure that all information in this book concerning drug dosages, schedules, and routes of administration is accurate as of the time of publication and consistent with standards set by the U.S. Food and Drug Administration and the general medical community. As medical research and practice advance, however, therapeutic standards may change. For this reason and because human and mechanical errors sometimes occur, we recommend that readers follow the advice of a physician who is directly involved in their care or the care of a member of their family.

Copyright © 1989 American Psychiatric Press, Inc.
ALL RIGHTS RESERVED
Manufactured in the United States of America
First Edition   92 91 90 89 4 3 2 1

The paper used in this publication meets the minimum requirements of the American National Standard for Information Sciences—Permanence of Paper for Printed Library Materials ANSI Z39.48-1984. ∞™

Library of Congress Cataloging-in-Publication Data

Current approaches to the prediction of violence / edited by David A. Brizer, Martha Crowner
        p.   cm.—(The Progress in psychiatry series)
    Includes bibliographies.
    ISBN 0-88048-289-3 (alk. paper)
    1. Violence—Forecasting. 2. Violence in psychiatric hospitals—Forecasting. I. Brizer, David A., 1953-
II. Crowner, Martha, 1956-   . III. Series.
    [DNLM: 1. Criminal Psychology. 2. Violence.
BF 575.A3 C976]
RC569.5.V55C87 1988
616.85'82—dc19
DNLM/DLC
for Library of Congress   88-7443
                                                              CIP

Contents

vii   Contributors

ix   Introduction to the *Progress in Psychiatry* Series
    David Spiegel, M.D.

xi   Introduction: Overview of Current Approaches to the Prediction of Violence
    David A. Brizer, M.D.

1   1   A Model for the Short-Term Prediction of Violence Potential
    Kenneth Tardiff, M.D., M.P.H.

13   2   Predicting Careers of Criminal Violence: Descriptive Data and Predispositional Factors
    Terrie E. Moffitt, Ph.D.
    Sarnoff A. Mednick, Dr. Med., Ph.D.
    William F. Gabrielli, Jr., M.D., Ph.D.

35   3   Prediction of Assaultive Behavior in Psychiatric Inpatients: Is It Possible?
    Antonio Convit, M.D.
    Judith Jaeger, Ph.D.
    Shang Pin Lin, Ph.D.
    Morris Meisner, Ph.D.
    Jan Volavka, M.D., Ph.D.

63   4   Clinical and Historical Correlates of
             Dangerous Inpatient Behavior
                 Jerome A. Yesavage, M.D.
                 David A. Brizer, M.D.

85   5   Hierarchical Neural Regulation of
             Aggression: Some Predictable Patterns
             of Violence
                 David M. Bear, M.D.

101 6   Environmental Concomitants of
             Psychiatric Inpatient Violence
                 Martha Crowner, M.D.

121 7   Child Abuse, Neglect, and Violent
             Criminal Behavior
                 Cathy Spatz Widom, Ph.D.

149 8   Inpatient Psychiatric Violence: Its
             Course and Associated
             Symptomatology
                 Menahem I. Krakowski, M.D., Ph.D.
                 Judith Jaeger, Ph.D.
                 Jan Volavka, M.D., Ph.D.

163 9   Schizophrenic Violence and
             Psychopathology
                 Menahem I. Krakowski, M.D., Ph.D.
                 Jan Volavka, M.D., Ph.D.

Contributors

David M. Bear, M.D.
Associate Professor of Psychiatry, Vanderbilt University School of Medicine; and Director of Neuropsychiatry, Vanderbilt University School of Medicine

David A. Brizer, M.D.
Research Assistant Professor of Psychiatry, New York University School of Medicine; Director of Alcoholism Treatment Clinic, Bellevue Hospital; New School for Social Research

Antonio Convit, M.D.
Research Assistant Professor of Psychiatry, New York University School of Medicine; and Research Director, Kirby Psychiatric Center

Martha Crowner, M.D.
Clinical Instructor of Psychiatry, New York University School of Medicine

William F. Gabrielli, Jr., M.D., Ph.D.
Department of Psychiatry, University of Kansas

Judith Jaeger, Ph.D.
Research Assistant Professor of Psychology, Department of Psychiatry, New York University School of Medicine

Menahem I. Krakowski, M.D., Ph.D.
Nathan S. Kline Institute for Psychiatric Research

Shang Pin Lin, Ph.D.
Nathan S. Kline Institute for Psychiatric Research

Sarnoff A. Mednick, Dr. Med., Ph.D.
Professor of Psychology, Social Science Research Institute, University of Southern California

Morris Meisner, Ph.D.
Associate Professor of Psychiatry, New York University School of Medicine

Terrie E. Moffitt, Ph.D.
Assistant Professor of Psychology, University of Wisconsin at Madison

Kenneth Tardiff, M.D., M.P.H.
Associate Professor of Public Health, Cornell University Medical
College

Jan Volavka, M.D., Ph.D.
Professor of Psychiatry, New York University School of Medicine;
Director of Research, Manhattan Psychiatric Center; and Chief,
Clinical Research Division, Nathan S. Kline Institute for Psychiatric
Research

Cathy Spatz Widom, Ph.D.
Professor of Criminal Justice and Psychology, Indiana University

Jerome A. Yesavage, M.D.
Associate Professor of Psychiatry and Behavioral Sciences, Stanford
University School of Medicine; and Director, Aging Clinical
Research Center, Veterans Administration Medical Center, Palo Alto

Introduction to the Progress in Psychiatry Series

The *Progress in Psychiatry* Series is designed to capture in print the excitement that comes from assembling a diverse group of experts from various locations to examine in detail the newest information about a developing aspect of psychiatry. This series emerged as a collaboration between the American Psychiatric Association's Scientific Program Committee and the American Psychiatric Press, Inc. Great interest was generated by a number of the symposia presented each year at the APA Annual Meeting, and we realized that much of the information presented there, carefully assembled by people who are deeply immersed in a given area, would unfortunately not appear together in print. The symposia sessions at the Annual Meetings provide an unusual opportunity for experts who otherwise might not meet on the same platform to share their diverse viewpoints for a period of three hours. Some new themes are repeatedly reinforced and gain credence, while in other instances disagreements emerge, enabling the audience and now the reader to reach informed decisions about new directions in the field. The *Progress in Psychiatry* Series allows us to publish and capture some of the best of the symposia and thus provide an in-depth treatment of specific areas which might not otherwise be presented in broader review formats.

Psychiatry is by nature an interface discipline, combining the study of mind and brain, of individual and social environments, of the humane and the scientific. Therefore, progress in the field is rarely linear—it often comes from unexpected sources. Further, new developments emerge from an array of viewpoints that do not necessarily provide immediate agreement but rather expert examination of the issues. We intend to present innovative ideas and data that will enable you, the reader, to participate in this process.

We believe the *Progress in Psychiatry* Series will provide you with an opportunity to review timely new information in specific fields of interest as they are developing. We hope you find that the excitement of the presentations is captured in the written word and that this book proves to be informative and enjoyable reading.

David Spiegel, M.D.
Series Editor
Progress in Psychiatry Series

Introduction: Overview of Current Approaches to the Prediction of Violence

Quite possibly the reader is wondering why yet another volume on the prediction of violence is necessary. After all, hasn't the question of whether we can predict violence been posed numerous times—and haven't numerous psychiatrists, psychologists, and criminologists repeatedly responded to this question in the negative?

Actually, this was the situation some 10 or 15 years ago, when the consensus of a number of studies was that, in general, clinicians could not accurately predict violence. At best, for every correct prediction one could count on two falsely positive ones as well (Cocozza and Steadman 1974).

However, the question of whether we can predict violence may itself suffer from methodological limitations (Shah 1981). Specifically, we need to recognize the complexity of the issue of prediction and to define the parameters of our inquiry. What types of violence, for example, are we interested in predicting? Over what period of time and in which situations will our predictions need to be made? What degree of sensitivity and specificity in our predictions represents an acceptable level of accuracy?

The aforementioned conclusion—that clinicians cannot accurately predict violence—was usually based on studies in which subjects were followed over long periods of time (often 1 year or longer). In addition, predictions made in one setting (typically, a psychiatric hospital) were meant to be relevant in an entirely different one, such as the community. Current prediction research, comprising a "second

The editors thank Susan Williams, without whose tireless enthusiasm and organizational skill this volume would not have been possible.

generation" (Monahan 1984) of studies that focus on time-limited, single-context forecasts, may in fact warrant optimism and justify the publication of a volume such as this.

Continued efforts at prediction on the part of researchers are not only justified but absolutely necessary, given the scope of the problem of violence today. In a recent workshop on violence and public health (Wolfgang 1986), homicide was noted to be the most likely cause of death for black males aged 15 to 24 in this country. In 1980, 24,000 homicide deaths were reported; in the same year, more than 1.5 million aggravated assaults of Americans aged 12 or older occurred. A survey of two large psychiatric state hospitals indicated that approximately 8 percent of the patients committed at least one physical assault within a period of 3 months (Tardiff and Sweillam 1982).

Further, predictions of dangerousness are routine components at many points in both the legal process and in decisions regarding involuntary commitment of psychiatric patients. Considering the enormous consequences of such predictions and the potential for their misapplication, prediction studies should be accorded priority in psychiatry and forensic research.

Although it is generally agreed that divergent definitions of violence are responsible in part for confounding attempts at prediction (Megargee 1969), few writers in the field have commented on the assumptions that are implicit in any such attempts. One such assumption is that "true" violence—violence that merits our serious attention and most energetic research efforts—is that which is visible and tangible. By this view, willfully (albeit indirectly) inflicted injury on persons in the form of corporate crime, industrial accidents, and environmental pollution would not be appropriately included in the purview of research on violence. Beyond this is the assumption that violence is a disease, or a disease-like phenomenon, with a specific etiology, pathogenesis, and treatment.

Studies in animals have succeeded in identifying a number of subtypes of aggressive behavior, each with its own distinct biological substrate (Goldstein 1974). Our ability to characterize the relevant etiological variables rests on our appreciation of the heterogeneous nature of human violent behavior.

There is, in fact, no single uniformly applicable definition of violence. Rather, the decisions regarding what constitutes violence, and what criteria for "dangerousness" are to be used in determining the necessity for, say, the continued preventive detention of individuals, are essentially political ones. An example of this is the singling out for preventive confinement of the mentally ill, despite the existence of many other groups of persons posing a significant danger to society (such as repeatedly drunken drivers and recidivistic criminal offenders) (Shah 1981). There is a very real conflict here between the goals of preservation of individual liberty (as in minimizing in our predictive decision rules the number of allowable false positive identifications of persons at risk for violence) and the maintenance of safety in society (Cohen et al. 1978). This conflict, some authors have argued (Cohen et al. 1978; Monahan 1981), is most appropriately resolved in the judicial or legislative sphere and not in the medical one.

An appreciation of the complexity of these issues serves as a starting point for clarifying our focus of study. The varieties of violence and contexts of violence described in this volume range from threats of harm verbalized by schizophrenic inpatients to unprovoked attacks by disinhibited individuals with brain damage to murders "processed" through the criminal justice system. What these behaviors have in common is the threat or application of force that results in physical injury to people (Monahan 1981). The criterion of intentionality included by some writers (e.g., Wolfgang 1981) in their definition of violence necessitates potentially unreliable judgments of states of mind of the violent individual.

The history of violence prediction in Anglo-American law has been described elsewhere (Dershowitz 1973). Although violent behavior has long been a focus of theory and treatment efforts in clinical psychology and psychiatry, it was not until the 1960s and 1970s that a number of correlational predictive studies began to appear. These studies—aptly described by Monahan (1984) as a "first generation" of prediction research—were characterized most often by univariate predictions intended to be valid over long periods of time and across different settings. An early and often-cited prototype of this kind of study identified a triad of childhood behaviors—enuresis, firesetting, and cruelty to animals—purported to be associated with "aggressive crime" in later life (Hellman and Blackman 1966). This finding was not replicated in a subsequent study (Climent and Ervin 1972).

A variety of factors have been reported to be correlates of violent behavior. These include dispositional variables (subdivided for the purpose of this discussion into "trait" and "state" predictors) and situational variables (Megargee 1976). Following a brief review of some of the relevant studies, it will be proposed that further investigation of the *interaction* between situational and dispositional variables will provide the basis for future, more successful efforts at violence prediction.

Trait Predictors

No significant association was found between age and assaultive or fear-inducing behavior prior to psychiatric hospitalization in a recent chart review of 1,687 patients (Rossi et al. 1986). This finding was consistent with the results of previous studies in which no significant association was demonstrated between age and the need for seclusion during hospitalization (Sepejak et al. 1983) or assaultive or fear-inducing behavior in the community (Sepejak et al. 1983; Soloff and Turner 1981). In other studies, however, assaultive patients were more likely to be younger than nonassaultive ones (Evenson et al. 1974; Harris and Varney 1986) and they were overrepresented among patients between the ages of 17 and 34 (Tardiff and Sweillam 1982). A retrospective survey of hospital incident reports generated over a 1-year period showed that, compared with the average daily inpatient population, assaultive patients were more likely to be younger than 45 years old (Pearson et al. 1986). Younger age was associated with the need for inpatient control measures (Tardiff 1983), with assaultive behavior prior to hospitalization (Tardiff and Sweillam 1980), and with assaultive behavior among psychiatric outpatients (Tardiff and Koenigsberg 1985). Younger age probably is an important correlate of assaultive behavior, although it is possible that age may interact with psychiatric diagnosis in the predisposition for violence.

The association between gender and violence is less clear and may depend on the specific context in which assaults are reported. Although a retrospective survey of hospital incident reports (Pearson et al. 1986) and charts (Rossi et al. 1986) showed that assaultive patients were more likely to be male, and a clear preponderance of males was noted in another study of hospital assaults (Evenson et al. 1974), other investigators failed to detect a gender difference between assaultive and nonassaultive inpatients (Tardiff and Sweillam 1980) or found a preponderance of females among psychiatric inpatients involved in assaults (Fottrell 1980). Males were more often involved in assaults preceding hospitalization (Lagos et al. 1977; Taintor 1980; Tardiff and Sweillam 1980) and in psychiatric outpatient assaults (Tardiff and Koenigsberg 1985), although this gender difference was not found in a study of preadmission violent behavior (Craig 1982) and in a study of dangerous behavior occurring during a 2-year follow-up of persons evaluated psychiatrically by court order (Sepejak et al. 1983).

The contribution of race toward assaultiveness remains ambiguous at present. Findings from inpatient studies include overrepresentation of nonwhites among intrainstitutional batterers (Depp 1982), more seclusion events among hospitalized black patients (Soloff and Turner 1981), higher risk of assaults in nonwhite patients (Depp 1982; Evenson et al. 1974; Steadman and Morrissey 1982), as well as lack of higher risk of assaultiveness in hospitalized nonwhites (Tardiff 1983) and greater frequency of danger-related inpatient events among whites (Lawson et al. 1984). The apparently increased rate of assaultiveness among nonwhites prior to admission disappears when the effect of diagnosis is controlled for. No differences in assault rates between blacks and whites as inpatients (Craig 1982; Tardiff and Sweillam 1980), as outpatients (Tardiff and Koenigsberg 1985), or preceding admission (Lagos et al. 1977) were noted in other studies. Black patients did not require the use of restraints in a psychiatric emergency service (Bell and Palmer 1983) or of emergency control measures while hospitalized (Tardiff 1983) significantly more often than white patients.

The relationship between educational level and assaultive behavior is similarly ambiguous. Although patients with lower educational levels were reported to have had more problems with assaultive behavior before hospital admission in one study (Tardiff and Sweillam 1980), no such association was found in another study (Rossi et al. 1986).

Correlations between patients' legal status and dangerousness have been noted in some studies. Patients with histories of violent offenses and of time spent in prison were more dangerous during a 24-month follow-up period than patients without such histories (Menzies et al. 1981). The finding that assaultive and fear-inducing patients were more likely to be admitted involuntarily than other patients has been noted by a number of investigators (Rofman et al. 1980; Rossi et al. 1986; Shore et al. 1981). Patients committed to a hospital because of "risk of physical harm to others" were more likely to assault someone during their hospitalization than were controls (Rofman et al. 1980).

In fact, a history of violent behavior has been shown by several observers (Monahan 1981; Steadman and Cocozza 1974) to be perhaps the best single "objective" indicator of future dangerousness (Menzies et al. 1981). Previous threats of assaults have been found to be associated with subsequent dangerous behavior as well (MacDonald 1963). The probability of assaultiveness increases with each additional previous act of violence in an individual (Shah 1978; Wolfgang 1978). Bipolar patients who had been violent prior to hospital admission were more likely to be assaultive than a comparison group without violent behavior before admission (Yesavage 1983a). In one study (Climent and Ervin 1972), there was no difference in violent criminal history between emergency room patients with and without presenting complaints of violence.

Greater lengths of stay on a maximum security ward (Harris and Varney 1986) and in a psychiatric hospital (Shader et al. 1977) have been reported as correlates of inpatient assaultiveness.

An extensive literature on personality variables associated with violence exists (Roberts et al. 1981). Investigators have attempted to characterize violent individuals by means of various psychometric tests such as the Wechsler Adult Intelligence Scale (Shawver and Jew 1978), the Rorschach (Purdue and Lester 1972), and the Thematic Apperception Test (Matranga 1976). One typology emerging from this kind of work has been that of the "overcontrolled" assaultive offender (Megargee 1966), who purportedly aggresses only after an accumulated series of provocations causes the overloading and breakdown of "strong generalized inhibitions" (Blackburn 1968). Minnesota Multiphasic Personality Inventory scores of extremely assaultive offenders indicated that this group was more overcontrolled than a comparison group of moderately assaultive offenders (Blackburn 1968).

Violent behavior appears to be a final common pathway for the expression of a variety of insults to the central nervous system (Mark and Ervin 1970; Monroe 1970). A history of alcoholic blackouts was associated with assaultiveness in a group of acute schizophrenic patients (Yesavage and Zarcone 1983).

An association between seizure disorders and violent behavior has been frequently reported, and much clinical and research interest in recent years has focused on the interictal behaviors of patients with complex partial seizures (see Chapter 5). In one study (Lewis et al. 1983), hospitalized homicidally aggressive children were more likely to have had a seizure than nonhomicidal controls. Patients described as having "episodic dyscontrol" (Bach-y-Rita 1974) had an increased frequency of seizure disorder, especially of the psychomotor type. Assaultive psychiatric inpatients (but not outpatients) had a greater likelihood of having seizure disorders than did nonassaultive patients (Tardiff 1983).

Inpatients with organic brain syndrome had a risk rate for assault that was twice as high as that reported for schizophrenics (Evenson et al. 1974). Violent prisoners showed significantly more brain dysfunction than nonviolent prisoners in their responses on a neuropsychological test battery (Spellacy 1978). Approximately 75 percent of 400 violent adult prisoners had histories of loss of consciousness resulting from head injuries (Mark and Ervin 1970). The association between the presence of neurological "soft signs" and conduct disorders in childhood is controversial; this association was not seen in one study (Shaffer et al. 1985) but has been demonstrated in others (Lewis et al. 1979; Wolff et al. 1982).

An association between assaultive and suicidal behavior has been frequently reported (Inamdar et al. 1982; Planansky and Johnston 1977; Tardiff and Sweillam 1980). Hospitalized homicidally aggressive children were significantly more likely to have attempted suicide compared to nonhomicidal controls (Lewis et al. 1983). Patients' scores on hostility ratings were significantly correlated with measures of self-destructive behavior on a psychiatric ward (Yesavage 1983b). Scars resulting from self-inflicted wounds were noted in 37 percent of a sample of habitually violent patient/inmates (Bach-y-Rita 1974), and violent patients frequently reported thoughts of suicide (Climent and Ervin 1972). Subjects presenting with complaints of violence to an emergency room more often had suicidal thoughts than did controls (Climent and Ervin 1972).

Parental psychiatric illness may be correlated with violent behavior; maternal psychiatric hospitalization was significantly more likely in homicidally aggressive children than in their nonhomicidal peers (Lewis et al. 1983). Violent patients may often relate histories of parental alcohol abuse (Climent and Ervin 1972).

Victimization of children and familial brutality (see Chapter 7) have been repeatedly reported as correlates of violence and violent crime in adulthood (Climent and Ervin 1972; MacDonald 1963; Mulvihill and Tumin 1969). Homicidally aggressive children frequently had fathers who were violent (Lewis et al. 1963). College students who received a high amount of corporal punishment as children were reported to be more aggressive and delinquent than students lacking such a history (Bryan and Freed 1982). Assaultive behavior of psychiatric inpatients was significantly correlated with measures of severity of parental discipline and degree of family conflict (Yesavage et al. 1983).

Increasing attention has been turned in recent years to the identification of possible biological trait markers of violent behavior. A difference in skin conductance (galvanic skin response) has been detected between nonpsychopaths and psychopaths and has been postulated as the physiological basis for the psychopath's increased risk of antisocial behavior (Mednick et al. 1982). More recent evidence (Witkin et al. 1976) has refuted earlier reports of disproportionate numbers of anomalous XYY chromosome–bearing men in maximum security hospitals. Biological researchers have reported lowered cerebrospinal fluid levels of a serotonin metabolite, 5-hydroxyindoleacetic acid, in individuals with histories of violence or particularly violent suicide attempts (Linnoila et al. 1983). The role of neurotransmitter status in violent behavior is being actively investigated at present.

State Predictors

It is likely that transient fluctuations of cognitive and physiological status—states—are at least as influential in determining violent behavior as are more enduring characteristics such as gender and race.

A chronically unsettled, persistently controversial focus of prediction research has been mental illness. Is the popular perception of the mentally ill—as a group given to outbursts of unprovoked violence that occur with greater frequency than is seen in the population at large—a valid one? The question is of particular importance because "The mentally ill are the only group in the United States who can be preventively detained for violence they might perpetrate rather than for violence they have performed" (Steadman 1981, p. 243).

Present-day researchers are constrained by ethical and medical-legal considerations from actually testing their predictions. Consider the consequences of releasing for investigative purposes half of a population of preventively detained inmates! Instead, prediction studies have relied on "experiments of nature," that is, situations in which judicial decisions have resulted in the release of involuntarily hospitalized psychiatric patients into the community. These studies, together with a number of surveys of the criminality (arrest records) of psychiatric patients, have by and large provided the basis for any conclusions heretofore reached on possible relationships between mental illness and violence.

The conclusion arrived at from a series of studies done in the 1950s and earlier was that released psychiatric patients had a lower rate of arrest for violent crime than did the general population (Zitrin et al. 1976). Studies conducted in the subsequent two decades showed an apparently higher rate of violent crime among former psychiatric patients (Giovannoni and Curel 1967; Rappaport and Lassen 1965; Zitrin et al. 1976). This discrepancy has been explained as resulting from the hospitalization in recent years of a disproportionate number of patients with multiple arrest records (Monahan 1981) and from an increased diversion of arrestees from the criminal justice system to psychiatric institutions (Zitrin et al. 1976).

In fact, a number of contemporary authorities have concluded that the rate of violent crime among the mentally ill is essentially similar to that of the general population (Climent and Ervin 1972; Cohen 1980; Rabkin 1979; Rappaport and Lassen 1965; Teplin 1985). There was no relationship between a history of prior psychiatric hospitalization and subsequent arrests in a cohort of released offenders (Steadman and Ribner 1980). Further, by comparison, ex-prisoners had subsequent arrest rates three to six times higher than those of ex-psychiatric patients (Steadman et al. 1978). On the other hand, one study (Sosowsky 1980) reported that released psychiatric patients without prior arrest records had arrest rates five times higher than that of the general population; a critic of this study pointed out that this conclusion was based on inappropriate baseline data (Teplin 1985).

Most of these studies suffer from serious methodological flaws, hence their attribution to a "first generation" (Monahan 1984) of prediction research. Arrest rates are not accurate indicators of true crime rates because all crimes do not result in arrest and because categories of crime reported in official records may be unrelated to the actual crimes committed. Other problems in these studies include the use of prior hospitalization as a criterion for mental illness and the reliance on state hospital patient populations in estimates of prevalence of violence among the mentally ill, which probably results in a bias toward overestimation of criminality (Teplin 1985). Further, the effects of institutionalization, pharmacotherapy, and the passage of time on outcome variables such as released patients' violence in the community have not been quantified and render interpretation of predictive data more difficult.

A related issue concerns whether mentally ill individuals with certain diagnoses are more at risk for violent behavior than those with other diagnoses. This issue, too, is by no means yet resolved; results of all relevant studies are not in agreement and many of the methodological criticisms leveled at studies of violence among the mentally ill are equally applicable to extant research on psychiatric diagnosis and violence.

Nonetheless, many investigators have concluded that a definite association does exist between the diagnosis of schizophrenia and violent behavior in a variety of settings (Pearson et al. 1986; Planansky and Johnston 1977; Shader et al. 1977; Tardiff and Sweillam 1980, 1982; Taylor and Gunn 1984). Other workers, it should be mentioned, have reported a relatively low risk for assault in schizophrenics, and instead have noted high risk for patients with personality disorder (Evenson et al. 1974; Ionno 1983). Whether paranoid schizophrenics are more violent than patients with other subtypes of schizophrenia is at present unresolved. Organic brain syndromes associated with psychosis and mental retardation have also been noted to increase the risk for inpatient assault. (Tardiff 1983).

A great deal of research effort has been aimed at elucidating possible correlations between type and severity of psychopathology and the occurrence of violence. Violent offenders have often been found to be actively psychotic at the time of committing their index offense (Lanzkron 1963; Taylor 1985; Taylor and Gunn 1984; Virkunnen 1974). High ratings of patients on particular items of rating scales such as the Brief Psychiatric Rating Scale (BPRS) have been found to be predictive of inpatient assaultiveness (Yesavage et al. 1981), and psychiatric inpatients have been classified on the basis of BPRS scores into "high-" and "low-visibility" subtypes (Tanke and Yesavage 1985) (see Chapter 4). An extensive review of the literature on psychiatric diagnosis and psychopathology and their relation to violent behavior (Krakowski et al. 1986) makes the point that parameters such as phase of illness and severity of psychopathology are significant determinants of outcomes of studies in these areas.

The effect of testosterone on male violence remains disputed. When compared with control subjects, male prisoners with histories of violent crime in general (Kreuz and Rose 1971), rapists (Rada et al. 1983), and delinquents with convictions for general violent crime (Schiavi et al. 1984) had higher blood testosterone levels. However, a recent review of studies on endocrine status and violence concluded by stating that most studies of testosterone levels in violent criminals and sex offenders failed to show marked differences from non-offender subjects (Coe and Levine 1983). These authors make the additional point that the few reports noting a positive correlation between testosterone level and violence may actually be documenting the effect of aggressive behavior on male hormone output (Coe and Levine 1983).

States of intoxication resulting from the ingestion of various drugs have been implicated in violent behavior. A number of studies have related alcohol intake to crime (Guze et al. 1962; Shuntich and Taylor 1972) and homicide (Felson and Steadman 1983). Although amphetamine use was found to have no relation to sexual or other violent crimes in at least one study (Blum 1969), others have reported such an association (Ellinwood 1971; Ervin and Lion 1969; Mulvihill and Tumin 1969). More recently, phencyclidine (PCP or "angel dust") has gained notoriety as a violence-promoting drug, but controlled studies have not been done to substantiate this impression.

Finally, marital status has been investigated as a possible correlate of violence. One recent study (Rossi et al. 1986) found no association between patients' marital status and assaultive or fear-inducing behavior occurring before hospital admission. Other investigators, however, have found that men and women who had never married were more likely to have been assaultive before admission (Taintor 1980; Tardiff and Sweillam 1980).

Situational Predictors

There is widespread agreement among those who study the prediction of violence that situational variables are crucial parameters of violent behavior (Depp 1976; Dietz and Rada 1982; Felson and Steadman 1983; Fottrell 1980). "To reach [a] nirvana of prediction, it is necessary for reseachers to begin the arduous task of compiling and verifying a catalog of situations that relate to the future occurrence of violent behavior" (Monahan 1981, p 93).

Numerous interactional and situational variables have been reported as correlates of violent behavior, including time of day (Depp 1982; Fottrell 1980), overcrowding (Straker et al. 1977), location (Dietz and Rada 1982), behavior of the victim (Felson and Steadman 1983), staff countertransference issues (Lion and Pasternak 1973), and even phases of the moon (Stokman 1984). (Chapter 6 provides a detailed discussion of situational variables that may be relevant to violent behavior.) Like the research on dispositional variables discussed previously, the studies to date on situational variables have yielded only limited insight into violent behavior because they have been mostly limited to reports of univariate descriptive statistics.

Prognosis for Prediction

Having come this far in surveying prediction efforts to date, what can be concluded about the ability of clinicians to forecast violence? Numerous authors have taken a rather pessimistic stance on the issue. Although some studies of variables used by mental health professionals to predict dangerousness are based at least in part on subjects' previous histories of violence (Konecni et al. 1980; Pfohl 1979), other studies have pointed to the influence of rater characteristics on the judgment of dangerousness (Stokman 1984). Some authors have questioned the utilization of mental health professionals in the service of implementing "social control measures" (Szasz 1963) and have emphasized the moral and political issues involved in relegating the prediction of violence to the mental health sphere (Monahan et al. 1979). A report by the American Psychiatric Association (1974) concluded that mental health professionals were not "competent to make such judgments." In *The Rights of Mental Patients: An American Civil Liberties Union Handbook*, Ennis and Emery (1978) stated that "predictions of dangerousness are wrong about 95% of the time."

These conclusions are based for the most part on studies (i.e.,

Kozol et al. 1972; Steadman and Cocozza 1974; Thornberry and Jacoby 1979) involving follow-up of released patient/offenders in a different setting (the community) over periods of time measured in years.

Many of these earlier prediction studies are based on clinicians' judgments of dangerousness rather than on forecasts derived from actuarial (statistical) tables. More recent attempts at prediction have incorporated the use of cross-validation samples (i.e., Menzies et al. 1985; Quinsey and Maguire 1986; Steadman and Morrissey 1982) and actuarial tables in an effort to improve predictive ability. Although this approach has not always met with success (Wenk et al. 1972), the discussion of some recent hospital- and community-based predictive studies in Chapter 3 reveals a general trend toward increased sensitivity and specificity of researchers' predictions.

Awareness of the methodological problems of past prediction studies points the way toward future efforts. Violent behavior is a multiply determined phenomenon and needs to be approached as such. Dispositional (state and trait) determinants are as relevant as situational and interactional ones in the genesis of the violent act. Identification of specific populations at particularly high risk for violence—such as multiple recidivists (Wolfgang et al. 1972)—appropriately addresses the low base rate issue and eases the predictive task. The combined use of clinical and actuarial data in the prediction of violence is certainly dictated by the weight of findings to date. Finally (and this point bears repetition), limiting predictions to shorter intervals of time and to single settings will result in greater predictive accuracy.

Having successfully negotiated his or her way this far, the reader is invited to peruse the following chapters for a more detailed view of some of the major facets of our present understanding of violent behavior and its prediction. Most of the material contained in this volume was originally presented as a symposium on the prediction of violence, held at the 1987 annual meeting of the American Psychiatric Association in Chicago. Because each of the symposium participants generously agreed to contribute chapters, it is possible for us to offer this extensive, multidisciplinary survey of current approaches to the prediction of violence.

Dr. Tardiff, whose work in psychiatric epidemiology has laid the groundwork for many of the current research efforts in prediction, discusses in Chapter 1 a number of variables correlated with violence committed by psychiatric patients; he then offers a model based on these correlates for the short-term prediction of violent behavior. Drs. Moffitt, Mednick, and Gabrielli (Chapter 2) describe the methodology and findings of a major study of the criminal careers of a large Danish birth cohort and relate aggression in adulthood to a number of central nervous system insults incurred early in life. The work of Drs. Convit, Jaeger, Lin, Meisner, and Volavka (Chapter 3) is perhaps prototypical of what may be anticipated as a "third generation" of violence research in its successful use of actuarial methods in the prediction of time-limited, single-context violence in state hospital patients. Other significant correlates of inpatient violence are described in Chapter 4 by Drs. Yesavage and Brizer, who offer a review of a number of important findings in studies conducted in this population and setting. Dr. Bear's work (Chapter 5) illuminates the contribution of the brain in various states of dysfunction and health to human violent behavior, clarifying the dispositional aspects of violent behavior referred to earlier. The situational components of violence are elucidated in a review by Dr. Crowner (Chapter 6) of studies relevant to the understanding of the role of setting in violent behavior. In Chapter 7, Dr. Widom reviews a number of studies on possible childhood antecedents (such as child abuse and neglect) of violent criminal behavior. Drs. Krakowski, Jaeger, and Volavka (Chapter 8) present a review of the literature on psychopathology and violence and describe their study of the association between ward functioning and violence among psychiatric inpatients. In Chapter 9, Drs. Krakowski and Volavka review the literature on violence among schizophrenic patients and discuss methodological issues relevant to research in this area.

I hope that this volume increases our understanding of violent behavior and stimulates further efforts at its prediction, containment, and prevention.

David A. Brizer, M.D.

REFERENCES

American Psychiatric Association: Clinical Aspects of the Violent Individual. Washington, DC, American Psychiatric Association, 1974

Bach-y-Rita G: Habitual violence and self-mutilation. Am J Psychiatry 131:1018–1020, 1974

Bell CC, Palmer J: Survey of demographic characteristics of patients requiring restraints in a psychiatric emergency room service. J Natl Med Assoc 75:981–987, 1983

Blackburn R: Personality in relation to extreme aggression in psychiatric offenders. Br J Psychiatry 114:821–828, 1968

Blum R: Drugs and violence, in Crimes of Violence: Staff Report to the National Commission on the Causes and Prevention of Violence, Vol 13, Append 32. Edited by Mulvihill D, Tumin M. Washington, DC, US Government Printing Office, 1969, pp 1461–1523

Bryan JW, Freed FW: Corporal punishment: normative data and sociological and psychological correlates in a community college population. Journal of Youth and Adolescence 11:77–87, 1982

Climent CE, Ervin FR: Historical data in the evaluation of violent subjects. Arch Gen Psychiatry 27:621–624, 1972

Cocozza JJ, Steadman HJ: Some refinements in the measurement and prediction of dangerous behavior. Am J Psychiatry 131:1012–1014, 1974

Coe CL, Levine S: Biology of aggression. Bull Am Acad Psychiatry Law 11:131–148, 1983

Cohen CI: Crime among mental patients: a critical analysis. Psychiatr Q 52:100–107, 1980

Cohen M, Groth A, Siegel R: The clinical prediction of dangerousness. Crime and Delinquency 24:28–39, 1978

Craig TJ: An epidemiologic study of problems associated with violence among psychiatric inpatients. Am J Psychiatry 139:1262–1266, 1982

Depp FC: Violent behavior patterns on psychiatric wards. Aggressive Behavior 2:295–306, 1982

Dershowitz A: Preventive confinement: a suggested framework for constitutional analysis. Texas Law Review 51:1277–1324, 1973

Dietz PE, Rada RT: Battery incidents and batterers in a maximum security hospital. Arch Gen Psychiatry 39:31–34, 1982

Ellinwood EH Jr: Assault and homicide associated with amphetamine abuse. Am J Psychiatry 127:1170–1175, 1971

Ennis B, Emery R: The Rights of Mental Patients: An American Civil Liberties Union Handbook. New York, Avon, 1978

Ervin FR, Lion JR: Clinical evaluation of the violent patient, in Crimes of Violence: Staff Report to the National Commission on the Causes and Prevention of Violence, Vol 13, Append 24. Edited by Mulvihill D, Tumin M. Washington, DC, US Government Printing Office, 1969, pp 1163–1188

Evenson RC, Sletten IW, Altman H, et al: Disturbing behavior: a study of incident reports. Psychiatr Q 48:266–275, 1974

Felson RB, Steadman HJ: Situational factors in disputes leading to criminal violence. Criminology 21:59–74, 1983

Fottrell E: A study of violent behavior among patients in psychiatric hospitals. Br J Psychiatry 136:216–221, 1980

Giovannoni J, Gurel L: Socially disruptive behavior of ex-mental patients. Arch Gen Psychiatry 17:146–153, 1967

Goldstein M: Brain research and violent behavior: a summary and evaluation of the status of biomedical research on brain and aggressive behavior. Arch Neurol 30:1–35, 1974

Guze SB, Tuason VB, Gatfield PD, et al: Psychiatric illness and crime with particular reference to alcoholism: a study of 233 criminals. J Nerv Ment Dis 134:512–521, 1962

Harris GT, Varney GW: A ten-year study of assaults and assaulters on a maximum security psychiatric unit. Journal of Interpersonal Violence 1:173–191, 1986

Hellman D, Blackman N: Enuresis, firesetting, and cruelty to animals: a triad predictive of adult crime. Am J Psychiatry 122: 1431–1435, 1966

Inamdar SC, Lewis DO, Siomopoulos G, et al: Violent and suicidal behavior in psychotic adolescents. Am J Psychiatry 139:932–935, 1982

Ionno JA: A prospective study of assaultive behavior in female psychiatric patients, in Assaults Within Psychiatric Facilities. Edited by Lion JR, Reid WH. New York, Grune & Stratton, 1983, pp 71–80

Konecni V, Mulcahy E, Ebbesen E: Prison or mental hospital: factors affecting the processing of persons suspected of being "mentally disorderd sex offenders," in New Direction in Psychological Research. Edited by Lipsitt P, Sales B. New York, Van Nostrand Reinhold, 1980

Kozol H, Boucher R, Garofalo R: The diagnosis and treatment of dangerousness. Crime and Delinquency 18:371–392, 1972

Krakowski M, Volavka J, Brizer D: Psychopathology and violence: a review of literature. Compr Psychiatry 27:131–148, 1986

Kreuz LE, Rose RM: Assessment of aggressive behavior and plasma testosterone in a young criminal population. Psychosom Med 34:321–332, 1971

Lagos J, Perlmutter K, Saexinger H: Fear of the mentally ill: empirical support for the common man's responses. Am J Psychiatry 134:1134–1137, 1977

Lanzkron J: Murder and insanity: a survey. Am J Psychiatry 119:754–758, 1963

Lawson WB, Yesavage JA, Werner PD: Race, violence, and psychopathology. J Clin Psychiatry 45:294–297, 1984

Lewis DO, Shanok SS, Pincus JH, et al: Violent juvenile delinquents. J Am Acad Child Psychiatry 18:307–319, 1979

Lewis DO, Shanok SS, Grant M, et al: Homicidally aggressive young children: neuropsychiatric and experiential correlates. Am J Psychiatry 140:148–153, 1983

Linnoila M, Virkkunen M, Scheinin M, et al: Low cerebrospinal fluid 5-hydroxyindoleacetic acid concentration differentiates impulsive from nonimpulsive violent behavior. Life Sci 33:2609–2614, 1983

Lion JR, Pasternak SA: Countertransference reactions to violent patients. Am J Psychiatry 130:207–210, 1973

MacDonald JM: The threat to kill. Am J Psychiatry 120:120–130, 1963

Mark VH, Ervin FH: Violence and the Brain. New York, Harper & Row, 1970

Matranga TT: The relationship between behavioral indices of aggression and hostile content on the TAT. J Pers Assess 40:130–143, 1976

Mednick SA, Pollock V, Volavka J, et al: Biology and violence, in Criminal Violence. Edited by Wolfgang ME, Weiner NA. Beverly Hills, Calif, Sage Publications, 1982

Megargee EI: Undercontrolled and overcontrolled personality types in extreme antisocial aggression. Psychological Monographs no 80, 1966

Megargee EI: The prediction of violence with psychological tests, in Crimes of Violence: Staff Report to the National Commission on the Causes and Prevention of Violence, Vol 13. Edited by Mulvihill D, Tumin M. Washington, DC, US Government Printing Office, 1969, pp 1016–1037

Megargee EI: The prediction of dangerous behavior. Criminal Justice Behavior 3:3–21, 1976

Menzies RH, Webster CD, Sepejak DS: Hitting the forensic sound barrier: predictions of dangerousness in a pretrial psychiatric clinic, in Dangerousness: Probability and Prediction, Psychiatry and Public Policy. Edited by Webster CD, Ben-Aron MH, Hucker SJ. Cambridge, Cambridge University Press, 1985, pp 115–144

Monahan J: The Clinical Prediction of Violent Behavior. Rockville, MD, US Department of Health and Human Services, 1981

Monahan J: The prediction of violent behavior: toward a second generation of theory and policy. Am J Psychiatry 141:10–15, 1984

Monahan J, Novaco R, Geis G: Corporate violence: research strategies for community psychology, in Challenges to the Criminal Justice System. Edited by Sarbin T. New York, Human Sciences, 1979

Monroe RR: Episodic Behavioral Disorders. Cambridge, MA, Harvard University Press, 1970

Mulvihill D, Tumin M (eds): Crimes of Violence: Staff Report to the National Commission on the Causes and Prevention of Violence. Washington, DC, US Government Printing Office, 1969

Pearson M, Wilmot E, Padi M: A study of violent behavior among inpatients in a psychiatric hospital. Br J Psychiatry 149:232–235, 1986

Perdue RL, Lester D: Personality characteristics of rapists. Percept Mot Skills 35:514, 1972

Pfohl SJ: From whom shall we be protected? Comparative approaches to the assessment of dangerousness. Int J Law Psychiatry 2:55–78, 1979

Planansky K, Johnston R: Homicidal aggression in schizophrenic men. Acta Psychiatr Scand 55:65–73, 1977

Quinsey VL, Maguire M: Maximum security psychiatric patients: actuarial and clinical prediction of dangerousness. Journal of Interpersonal Violence 1:143–171, 1986

Rabkin J: Criminal behavior of discharged mental patients: a critical reappraisal of the research. Psychol Bull 86:1–27, 1979

Rada RT, Laws DR, Kellner R, et al: Plasma androgens in violent and nonviolent sex offenders. Bull Am Acad Psychiatry Law 11:149–158, 1983

Rappaport J, Lassen G: Dangerousness-arrest rate comparisons of discharged patients and the general population. Am J Psychiatry 121:776–783, 1965

Roberts TK, Mock LAT, Johnstone EE: Psychological aspects of the etiology of violence, in Violence and the Violent Individual. Edited by Hays JR, Roberts TK, Solway KS. New York, SP Medical & Scientific Books, 1981, pp 9–34

Rofman ES, Askinazi C, Fant E: The prediction of dangerous behavior in emergency civil commitment. Am J Psychiatry 137:1061–1064, 1980

Rossi AM, Jacobs M, Monteleone M, et al: Characteristics of psychiatric patients who engage in assaultive or other fear-inducing behaviors. J Nerv Ment Dis 174:154–160, 1986

Schiavi RC, Theilgaard A, Owen DR, et al: Sex chromosome anomalies, hormones, and aggressivity. Arch Gen Psychiatry 41:93–99, 1984

Sepejak D, Menzies RJ, Webster CD, et al: Clinical prediction of dangerousness: two-year follow-up of 408 pre-trial forensic cases. Bull Am Acad Psychiatry Law 11:173–181, 1983

Shader RI, Jackson AH, Harmatz JS, et al: Patterns of violent behavior among schizophrenic inpatients. Diseases of the Nervous System 1:13–16, 1977

Shaffer D, Schonfeld I, O'Connor PA, et al: Neurological soft signs: their relationship to psychiatric disorder and intelligence in childhood and adolescence. Arch Gen Psychiatry 42:342–351, 1985

Shah SA: Dangerousness: a paradigm for exploring some issues in law and psychology. Am Psychol 33:224–238, 1978

Shah SA: Dangerousness: conceptual, prediction, and public policy issues, in Violence and the Violent Individual. Edited by Hays JR, Roberts TK, Solway KS. New York, SP Medical & Scientific Books, 1981, pp 151–178

Shawver L, Jew C: Predicting violent behavior from WAIS characteristics: a replication failure. J Consult Clin Psychol 46:206, 1978

Shore JH, Breakey W, Arvidson B: Morbidity and mortality in the commitment process. Arch Gen Psychiatry 38:930–934, 1981

Shuntich RJ, Taylor SP: Effects of alcohol on human aggression. Journal of Experimental Research in Personality 6:34–38, 1972

Soloff PH, Turner SM: Patterns of seclusion: a prospective study. J Nerv Ment Dis 169:37–44, 1981

Sosowsky L: Explaining the increased arrest rate among mental patients: a cautionary note. Am J Psychiatry 137:1602–1605, 1980

Spellacy F: Neuropsychological discrimination between violent and non-violent men. J Clin Psychol 34:49–52, 1978

Steadman HJ: Special problems in the prediction of violence among the mentally ill, in Violence and the Violent Individual. Edited by Hays JR, Roberts TK, Solway KS. New York, SP Medical & Scientific Books, 1981, pp 243–254

Steadman H, Cocozza JJ: Careers of the Criminally Insane. Lexington, Mass, Lexington Books, 1974

Steadman HJ, Morrissey JP: Predicting violent behavior: a note on a cross-validation study. Social Forces 61:475–483, 1982

Steadman HJ, Ribner SA: Changing perceptions of the mental health needs of inmates in local jails. Am J Psychiatry 137:1115–1116, 1980

Steadman HJ, Vandewyst D, Ribner SA: Comparing arrest rates of mental patients and criminal offenders. Am J Psychiatry 135:1218–1220, 1978

Stokman CLJ: Dangerousness and violence in hospitalized mentally ill offenders. Psychiatr Q 56:138–143, 1984

Straker M, Carman P, Fulton J: Assaultive behaviors in an institutional setting. Psychiatr J Univ Ottawa 2:185–190, 1977

Szasz T: Law, Liberty, and Psychiatry. New York, Macmillan, 1963

Tanke ED, Yesavage JA: Characteristics of assaultive patients who do and do not provide visible cues of potential violence. Am J Psychiatry 142:1409–1413, 1985

Tardiff K: A survey of assault by chronic patients in a state hospital system, in Assaults Within Psychiatric Facilities. Edited by Lion JR, Reid WH. New York, Grune & Stratton, 1983

Tardiff K, Koenigsberg HW: Assaultive behavior among psychiatric outpatients. Am J Psychiatry 142:960–963, 1985

Tardiff K, Sweillam A: Assault, suicide, and mental illness. Arch Gen Psychiatry 37:164–169, 1980

Tardiff K, Sweillam A: The occurrence of assaultive behavior among chronic psychiatric inpatients. Am J Psychiatry 139:212–215, 1982

Taylor PJ: Motives for offending among violent and psychotic men. Br J Psychiatry 147:491–498, 1985

Taylor PH, Gunn J: Violence and psychosis, I: risk of violence among psychotic men. Br Med J 288;1945–1949, 1984

Teplin LA: The criminality of the mentally ill: a dangerous misconception. Am J Psychiatry 142:593–599, 1985

Thornberry T, Jacoby J: The Criminally Insane: A Community Follow-Up of Mentally Ill Offenders. Chicago, University of Chicago Press, 1979

Virkkunen M: Observations on violence in schizophrenia. Acta Psychiatr Scand 50:145–151, 1974

Wenk E, Robison J, Smith G: Can violence be predicted? Crime and Delinquency 18:393–402, 1972

Witkin H, Mednick S, Schulsinger F, et al: Criminality in XYY and XXY men. Science 193:547–555, 1976

Wolff PH, Waber D, Bauermeister M, et al: The neuropsychological status of adolescent delinquent boys. J Child Psychol Psychiatry 23:267–279, 1982

Wolfgang M: An overview of research into violent behavior. Unpublished testimony before the U.S. House of Representatives Committee on Science and Technology, 1978

Wolfgang M: Sociocultural overview of criminal violence, in Violence and the Violent Individual. Edited by Hays JR, Robert TK, Solway KS. New York, SP Medical & Scientific Books, 1981

Wolfgang M: Interpersonal violence and public health care: new directions, new challenges, in Surgeon General's Workshop on Violence and Public Health Report. Leesburg, VA, Health Resources and Services Administration, 1986

Wolfgang M, Figlio R, Sellin T: Delinquency in a Birth Cohort. Chicago, University of Chicago Press, 1972

Yesavage JA: Correlates of dangerous inpatient behavior. Br J Psychiatry 143:554–557, 1983a

Yesavage JA: Relationships between measures of direct and indirect hostility and self-destructive behavior by hospitalized schizophrenics. Br J Psychiatry 143:173–176, 1983b

Yesavage JA, Zarcone V: History of drug abuse and dangerous behavior in inpatient schizophrenics. J Clin Psychiatry 44:259–261, 1983

Yesavage JA, Werner PD, Becker J: Inpatient evaluation of aggression in psychiatric patients. J Nerv Ment Dis 169:299–302, 1981

Yesavage JA, Becker JMT, Werner PD, et al: Family conflict, psychopathology, and dangerous behavior by schizophrenic inpatients. Psychiatry Res 8:271–280, 1983

Zitrin A, Hardesty AS, Burdock FI, et al: Crime and violence among mental patients. Am J Psychiatry 133:142–149, 1976

Chapter 1

A Model for the Short-Term Prediction of Violence Potential

Kenneth Tardiff, M.D., M.P.H.

Chapter 1

A Model for the Short-Term Prediction of Violence Potential

The prediction of violent behavior by psychiatrists (and other mental health professionals) is controversial, with some of these professionals maintaining that we have no greater expertise in this area than an intelligent layperson. Yet the public, and the courts in particular, believe psychiatrists should be able to predict whether a patient will be a danger to others for purposes of protecting potential victims of violence (Beck 1985).

This author maintains that a well-trained psychiatrist or other mental health professional should be able to predict a patient's short-term violence potential using assessment techniques analogous to the short-term predictors of suicide potential. *Short term* is defined as a period of a few days or a week at most, until the patient is seen for the next therapy session or aftercare/follow-up appointment. Beyond that time there is an opportunity for many intervening factors, as in the case of the stabilized schizophrenic patient stopping neuroleptic medication or the abstinent spouse abuser resuming drinking again. The author will present his model for the short-term prediction of violence potential as well as some of the research evidence supporting it, mostly citing his research since other authors are covered elsewhere in this book. As with prediction of suicide, one focuses on the clinical aspects of the evaluation, namely psychopathology, and one must take into consideration demographic, historical, and environmental factors that may be related to an increased risk of violence or suicide.

MODEL FOR THE SHORT-TERM PREDICTION OF VIOLENCE POTENTIAL

The evaluation of a patient's violence potential is done when a decision must be made in terms of whether to admit or not to admit a patient to a hospital in the emergency room or in the outpatient

3

office in *Tarasoff*-like situations, with duty to protect potential victims of one's patients. Of course this evaluation is made also at the time one is considering discharging a patient from the hospital. In making a decision about violence potential, one should interview the patient as well as family members, police, and other persons with information about the patient and violent incidents to guard against the patient minimizing dangerousness. One should review old charts for previous episodes of violence as well as arrest records and other records of judicial proceedings if available.

Asking About Violence

The evaluation of homicide potential is analogous to that of suicide potential. Even if the patient does not express thoughts of violence, one should routinely ask as part of every evaluation the subtle question "Have you ever lost your temper?" If the answer is yes, then the evaluator should proceed in terms of how, when, and so on in the same manner one would check for suicide potential with the question "Have you ever felt that life was not worth living?" If the answer is yes, one would proceed with the evaluation of the patient's potential for violence.

Appearance of the Patient

The appearance of the patient may prompt further scrutiny of the potential for violence. This includes the loud, agitated, angry-appearing patient who is impatient and refuses to comply with the usual intake procedures in the emergency room or clinic as well as the quiet, guarded patient who requires careful listening to for subtle violent ideation. Dysarthria, unsteady gait, dilated pupils, tremors, and other signs of acute drug or alcohol intoxication dictate caution and serious consideration of the patient's potential for violence, even though threats of violence may not be expressed.

How Well Planned Is the Threat?

Along the same lines as the evaluation of suicide potential, evaluation of violence potential includes ascertaining how well planned the threat is. Vague threats of killing someone are not as serious, all things being equal, as saying "I'm going to kill my wife because she is having an affair with the dentist."

Available Means

As with the suicide, the availability of a means of inflicting injury is important. For example, if the patient has recently purchased or owns a gun, one should obviously take the threat more seriously. If a weapon can be confiscated, this reduces the potential for homicide.

Past History of Violence or Impulsivity

A past history of violence or other impulsive behavior is often predictive of future violence. One should ask about injuries to other persons, destruction of property, suicide attempts, reckless driving, reckless spending, criminal offenses, sexual acting out, an impulsive behaviors. The author has found that violent pati mitted to public hospitals were more likely than nonviolent p. ...ts to have a history of prior arrests and violence (Tardiff and Sweillam 1980). Furthermore, in studies of admissions to public and private hospitals, a history of prior suicide attempts was found in a greater proportion for violent patients compared to nonviolent patients (Tardiff 1984; Tardiff and Sweillam 1980). Basic research has suggested that suicide and externally directed violence may share the same mechanisms in the brain that produce impulsivity. Brown et al. (1979, 1982) found that a history of aggressive behavior and a history of suicidal behavior were both related to decreased cerebrospinal fluid (CSF) 5-hydroxyindoleacetic acid (5-HIAA) levels. Lindberg et al. (1985) studying the CSF–5-HIAA levels in a group of men convicted of criminal homicide and a group of men who attempted suicide, found that these groups had lower levels of 5-HIAA in spinal fluid than did male controls. Linnoila et al. (1983) found that impulsive offenders had significantly lower CSF–5-HIAA concentrations than nonimpulsive offenders, the latter group defined as those who had premeditated their crimes. This is in agreement with other studies of suicide and serotonin metabolism (Linkowski 1985).

One should assess the degree of past injuries (e.g., broken bones and lacerations), as well as the identity of persons toward whom violence has been directed and the circumstances of such behavior. Often there is a pattern of past violent behavior in specific circumstances, for example, escalation of a dispute between a husband and wife or parent and child about issues of money, esteem, or sexuality. Unlike suicide, the presence of others at home may not tip the balance toward safety, but rather may increase the propensity toward violence unless the dynamics of past violent episodes are explored and prevented.

A past history of being abused as a child or being in a family where physical abuse occurred should be sought. Kempe and Helfer (1980) have reported that being abused as a child is related to becoming a physically abusive adult (i.e., a child abuser or otherwise violent adult). There is evidence that not only is being abused as a child related to adult violence, but that witnessing intrafamily violence (e.g., spouse abuse) is also related to increased problems with violence among children, especially boys, such as being hyperactive, cruel, bullying, and having temper tantrums (Jaffe et al. 1986). Likewise a history of obstetrical complications or subsequent head injury should be explored.

Alcohol and Drug Use

Alcohol and drug use should be assessed. Substances that can produce violent behavior include alcohol, barbiturates, other sedatives, and minor tranquilizers (as a result of the intoxicated state as well as during withdrawal). Other substances that can produce violence when the patient is intoxicated include amphetamines and other sympathomimetics, cocaine, phencyclidine (PCP) and other hallucinogens, anticholinergics, glue, other solvent/inhalants, and other drugs such as steroids. One should look for dysarthria, nystagmus, unsteady gait, dilated pupils, tachycardia, and tremors, all of which may indicate that a substance abuse disorder is present.

There are a number of epidemiological studies that have found a strong link between alcohol use and certain types of homicide involving disputes (Goodman et al. 1986; Tardiff et al. 1986). A number of street drugs of abuse are found to be associated with violent behavior, including amphetamines, cocaine, hallucinogens, and minor tranquilizers-sedatives (Menuck 1983; Nurno et al. 1985). Among men newly incarcerated in prison in Britain, Taylor and Gunn (1984) found 8.6 percent manifested acute withdrawal from alcohol or drugs and many had a history of alcohol and/or drug abuse. The pharmacological effect of disinhibition or withdrawal (in the case of alcohol and sedatives), and of excitement, disorganization, and delusional thinking (in the case of cocaine, amphetamines, and some hallucinogens) are important contributing factors to some violent episodes.

Other Organic Mental Disorders

Organicity increases the risk of violence. Central nervous system disorders that have been associated with violent behavior include traumatic brain injuries, intracranial infections including encephalitis and postencephalitic syndrome, tumors, partial complex seizures, cerebrovascular disorders, Alzheimer's disease, Wilson's disease, multiple sclerosis, and normal pressure hydrocephalus. Some systemic disorders affecting the central nervous system include metabolic disorders such as hypoglycemia, electrolyte imbalances, hypoxia, uremia,

Cushing's disease, vitamin deficiencies (as in pernicious anemia), systemic infections, systemic lupus erythematosus, porphyria, and industrial poisons (such as lead). In the author's public and private admission studies as well as in his study of violence among patients who were in state hospitals for years, many violent patients had chronic organic impairment of the brain related to chronic alcoholism, trauma, cerebrovascular disease, infection, Alzheimer's disease, and other gross brain disorders. Few episodes of violent behavior were associated with seizure disorders except for patients residing in the state hospitals for long periods of time and few in any setting were related to partial complex seizures (Tardiff 1984; Tardiff and Sweillam 1980, 1982).

The role of gross organic impairment in violence in other populations has been studied. Lewis et al. (1982) found that among delinquent, adolescent boys in correctional schools, a number had partial complex seizures and that the more violent boys were those with this disorder. Five boys committed violent acts during seizures, but violence was interictal as well. The violent boys with partial complex seizures were more likely to report impaired or distorted memory and to have low IQs, a frequent history of head trauma, and paranoid ideation and/or hallucinations, all of which were associated with poor impulse control and were not directly related to seizures. Devinsky and Bear (1984) emphasized the importance of epilepsy and subtle neurophysiological dysfunction in violence and illustrated various forms of violence that one may encounter through the use of case histories.

Psychosis

As with suicide, the presence of psychosis should make one take threats of violence very seriously and makes the assessment of violence potential essential, even if threats are not apparent.

In studies of patients admitted to public and private hospitals, schizophrenic patients represented a large proportion of patients admitted and were even greater in the group of violent patients (Tardiff 1984; Tardiff and Sweillam 1980). Both paranoid and nonparanoid schizophrenic patients were at increased risk of violence just prior to admission. In the study of private hospitals, there were adequate numbers of manic patients admitted to say that this group of patients also was at higher risk of violent behavior just before admission. In the study of patients residing in state hospitals for years, only the nonparanoid schizophrenic patients were at increased risk of violence in these hospitals and these violent patients manifested severe psychotic symptomatology (Tardiff and Sweillam 1982). Paranoid schizophrenic patients residing in these hospitals were more likely to be in the nonviolent group. Furthermore, a subsequent analysis showed that paranoid schizophrenic patients who had manifested violence in hospitals just prior to the survey were more likely than other previously violent patients to be deemed appropriate for community placement. It was apparent that the paranoid patients responded to medication and had decreased psychopathology related to violence, or at least they stopped talking about it and controlled themselves (Tardiff 1981).

The paranoid schizophrenic patient poses a number of problems. First of all, paranoid delusions may not be obvious; they may be very subtle or the patient may attempt to hide them. The evaluator must listen for subtle clues and should follow up regarding the assessment of violence toward others. Another problem with violent paranoid schizophrenic patients is that of noncompliance with medication once they have been stabilized. Other types of schizophrenics have more disorganized symptomatology; violence may be the result of that or of delusional or hallucinatory symptoms, particularly command hallucinations. Manics can also be disorganized and less intentional in terms of their violent behavior. Depressed patients are rarely violent; it is usually the patients who have psychotic depressions (and who murder their spouse and/or children and then commit suicide) who are violent.

Personality Disorder

In the author's study of patients admitted to public hospitals, assaultive patients were increased proportional to nonassaultive patients in the category "other disorders," which were predominantly personality disorders (Tardiff and Sweillam 1980). The most solid connection between violence and personality disorders was found in the study of patients coming to outpatient clinics at two private hospitals (Tardiff and Koenigsberg 1985).

Personality disorders particularly prone to violence include the explosive (organic), borderline, and antisocial personality disorders. With the organic personality or intermittent explosive disorder, there are several discrete episodes of loss of control involving violence toward others or destruction of property. A violent episode may have little apparent precipitating cause or may be linked to predictable patterns of escalation of conflict between the patient and others (usually family members). In any case, violence is out of proportion to any precipitating factors. The violence may occur for a few minutes or an hour and is often associated with alcohol use. It is followed by remorse and feelings of guilt concerning the beating of a spouse or child or other family member. Between episodes there are few problems with impulse control or violence.

This is in distinction to the antisocial personality, where there also are intermittent episodes of violent behavior. Between these violent outbursts there is pervasive antisocial behavior without remorse (e.g., theft, drug dealing, job problems, lying, and reckless driving). Differing from the intermittent explosive disorder, the borderline personality manifests in addition to episodic violence a broad instability of interpersonal relationships as well as profound mood and identity problems. Violence is just one of many impulsive behaviors, others being sexual acting out, overspending, overeating, suicide attempts, and drug and alcohol abuse.

Demographic Characteristics

Patients with increased risk of violence are often young, male, and derive from environments where there is poverty, disruption of families, and decreased social control (where violence is a more acceptable means of attaining a goal than in other segments of society).

In the author's study of patients admitted to public and private hospitals, as well as of those presenting to the outpatient clinics, there was an increased rate of assault among young patients. This was especially true for males under 20 years of age and for females under 34 years of age. (Tardiff 1982; Tardiff and Koenigsberg 1985; Tardiff and Sweillam 1980). In the studies of admission to public and private hospitals, patients 65 years of age and older were more likely than the middle-aged patients, but not as much as the younger patients, to have manifested assaultive behavior before admission. There was usually gross organic impairment in these older patients, with increased impulsivity and disorganization. Most of the violent episodes were not severe in terms of causing injury. In another study of patients admitted to a geriatric unit of a state hospital, Petrie (1982) found that approximately 8 percent of these patients committed serious violent acts with a weapon, usually a gun, and another 63 percent were physically assaultive without a weapon or verbally abusive toward other persons. For those geriatric patients using a weapon, it usually was their first violent episode and first experience with psychiatric treatment. Often, the violent acts were a result of paranoid delusions and were directed toward imagined persecutors. Those who did not use weapons differed from those using weapons in that a greater proportion of them had organic brain syndrome accompanied by a clouded sensorium. Their violence was usually not dangerous and was probably the result of disorganization and frustration rather than paranoid delusions.

In the author's two admission studies and the outpatient study, men were at least twice as likely as women to be violent. There was one exception. In the study of patients in hospitals for long periods of time, there was no difference in frequency of assault between male and female patients. This runs counter to what happens in society in general in terms of men being responsible for the bulk of violent crime. Numerous studies have shown that physical aggression is considered more "appropriate" for males in our society (Maccoby and Jacklin 1974). The absence of sex difference in hospitals may suggest that a blurring of sex-role differences occurs once a person becomes a chronic patient in a mental hospital. Mental status and age may be more important than sex in determining whether a chronic patient strikes out at other persons in the hospital.

The author has not found race itself to be a factor associated with increased risk of assault among psychiatric patients when socio-economic variables and education are taken into consideration (Tardiff and Sweillam 1980). Instead, the environment from which the patient comes must be considered in the determination of violence potential: is it one that views violence as an accepted means of obtaining what one wants in the face of poverty or lack of other legitimate means, education, work, and verbal skills (Messner and Tardiff 1985)?

SUMMARY

The assessment of violence potential for the short term (that is, in days or within a week) is analogous to the assessment of suicide potential. The clinician must consider the following:

- Subtle questioning of the patient if violence is not mentioned
- Appearance of the patient
- How well planned a threat of violence is
- Available means of inflicting injury
- Past history of violence and impulsive behavior with attention to frequency, degree of past injuries to others and self, and toward whom and under what circumstances
- Past history of abuse as a child and of witnessing domestic violence
- Alcohol and drug use
- Presence of organic mental disorders
- Presence of certain personality and impulse control disorders
- Demographic characteristics of the patient

All of these factors are weighed in the final assessment of whether the patient poses a significant risk to others and whether some action is necessary on the part of the evaluator. Action may include changing the treatment plan, hospitalizing the patient, or warning the intended victim and/or the police. All of the data on which the decision that the patient is or is not a risk for violence is based must be *documented in writing*, and the thinking process through which the decisions were made should be evident in the written documentation. Reassessment of violence potential should be made at short intervals (e.g., from visit to visit or every few days) if the patient is to continue to be treated outside the hospital or other institution. Clinicians have not been faulted for inaccurate prediction but for failure to collect data necessary for the prediction of violence and to logically use the data to make a prediction.

Although this model is sufficient in defining the basic components and process for the short-term evaluation of violence potential, it should be regarded as a concept useful for the time being and should be subjected to assessment through future research, as should the evaluation of suicide potential.

REFERENCES

Beck JC: The Potentially Violent Patient and the Tarasoff Decision in Psychiatric Practice. Washington, DC, American Psychiatric Press, 1985

Brown GL, Goodwin FK, Ballenger JC, et al: Aggression in humans correlates with cerebrospinal fluid amine metabolites. Psychiatry Res 1:131–139, 1979

Brown GL, Ebert MH, Goyer PF, et al: Aggression, suicide and serotonin: relationship to CSF amine metabolites. Am J Psychiatry 136:741–746, 1982

Devinsky O, Bear D: Varieties of aggressive behavior in temporal lobe epilepsy. Am J Psychiatry 141: 651–656, 1984

Goodman RA, Mercy JA, Loya F, et al: Alcohol use and interpersonal violence: alcohol detected in homicide victims. Am J Public Health 76:144–149, 1986

Jaffe P, Wolfe D, Wilson SK, et al: Family violence and child adjustment: a comparative analysis of girls' and boys' behavioral symptoms. Am J Psychiatry 143:74–77, 1986

Kempe CH, Helfer R (eds): The Battered Child Syndrome (3rd ed). Chicago, University of Chicago Press, 1980

Lewis DO, Pincus JH, Shanok SS, et al: Psychomotor epilepsy and violence in a group of incarcerated adolescent boys. Am J Psychiatry 139:882–887, 1982

Lindberg L, Tuck JR, Asberg M, et al: Homicide, suicide and CSF 5-HIAA. Acta Psychiatr Scand 71:230–236, 1985

Linkowski P: Editorial: suicide and biochemistry. Biol Psychiatry 20:123–134, 1985

Linnoila M, Virkkunen M, Scheinin M, et al: Low cerebrospinal fluid 5-hydroxindoleacetic acid concentration differentiates impulsive from nonimpulsive violent behavior. Life Sci 33:2609–2614, 1983

Maccoby EM, Jacklin CN: The Psychology of Sex Differences. Stanford, Calif, Stanford University Press, 1974

Menuck M: Clinical aspects of dangerous behavior. Journal of Psychiatry and the Law 11:277–304, 1983

Messner S, Tardiff K: Economic inequality and levels of homicide: an analysis of urban neighborhoods. Criminology 23:241–267, 1985

Nurco DN, Ball JC, Shaffer JW, et al: The criminality of narcotic addicts. J Nerv Ment Dis 173:94–102, 1985

Petrie J: Violence in geriatric patients. JAMA 248:443–448, 1982

Tardiff K: Assault in hospitals and placement in the community. Bull Am Acad Psychiatry Law 9:33–39, 1981

Tardiff K: Characteristics of assaultive patients in private psychiatric hospitals. Am J Psychiatry 141:1232–1235, 1984

Tardiff K, Koenigsberg HW: Assaultive behavior among psychiatric outpatients. Am J Psychiatry 142:960–963, 1985

Tardiff K, Sweillam A: Assault, suicide, and mental illness. Arch Gen Psychiatry 37:164–169, 1980

Tardiff K, Sweillam A: The occurrence of assaultive behavior among chronic psychiatric inpatients. Am J Psychiatry 139:212–215, 1982

Tardiff K, Gross E, Messner S: A study of homicide in Manhattan, 1981. Am J Public Health 76:139–143, 1986

Taylor PH, Gunn J: Violence and psychosis, I: risk of violence among psychotic men. Br Med J 288:1945–1949, 1984

Chapter 2

Predicting Careers of Criminal Violence: Descriptive Data and Predispositional Factors

Terrie E. Moffitt, Ph.D.
Sarnoff A. Mednick, Dr. Med., Ph.D.
William F. Gabrielli, Jr., M.D., Ph.D.

Chapter 2

Predicting Careers of Criminal Violence: Descriptive Data and Predispositional Factors

This chapter describes our recent efforts to identify both epidemiological and developmental factors that are predictive of violent criminal offending. It begins with a descriptive study of the criminal careers of 735 men charged with violent crimes, who are members of a Danish total birth cohort of 31,436 males. To identify aspects of a criminal career that may predict violent offending, we examined several aspects of their criminal careers: (1) their types of violent offenses, (2) the disproportionate amounts of crime committed by these violent men relative to their small number, (3) specialization in violent offending, (4) the relation between their violence and general criminal recidivism, and (5) the relation between age factors and later violence. Early onset of offending, chronic criminal recidivism, and being between the ages of 18 and 25 are identified as epidemiological predictors of eventual violent arrest.

The second half of the chapter presents our search for additional predictors of violence among early human developmental factors. Our study of the violent men in the Danish cohort had provided evidence for some specialization in violent offenses, even among juvenile offenders. Also, there is a literature demonstrating that aggressive behavior is a consistent pattern in some males from early

Preparation of this chapter was supported by U.S. Public Health Service Grant No. 1 R23 MH-42723-01 from the Antisocial and Violent Behavior Branch of the National Institute of Mental Health to the first author, and by a Research Scientist Award (Grant No. 1 K05 MH 00619-01) from the U.S. Department of Health, Education, and Welfare, Public Health Service, Alcohol, Drug Abuse, and Mental Health Administration to the second author.

15

childhood. Together these findings suggest that some factors operating very early in life may contribute to emergence of persistent violent behavior. Among such early factors are heritability and perinatal health. We describe an adoption study of criminal violence and a study of the association between minor physical anomalies (indices of disturbed fetal development) and perinatal birth complications and later arrest for violent crime. The chapter ends with the hypothesis that some agents operate very early in life to compromise central nervous system control of aggressive impulses; contribute to a picture of early-onset, consistent aggressiveness; and generalize to high frequency of nonviolent as well as violent antisocial behavior in young adulthood.

DESCRIPTION OF VIOLENCE CAREERS IN A LARGE BIRTH COHORT

Subjects and Methods

The cohort. This investigation examined data from all violent offenders in a true birth cohort comprised of the 31,436 male offspring born between January 1, 1944 and December 31, 1947 to mothers who were residents of Copenhagen, Denmark. The cohort was originally defined by Witkin et al. (1976). Use of such a large unselected cohort of subjects assures accurate representativeness of findings, and guarantees a full range of recorded offenses.

The criminality data. We were able to obtain complete information regarding official records of criminal behavior for 28,879 of the cohort members who were still alive at the time of data collection in 1974. Witkin et al. (1976) describe attrition in detail; almost all losses resulted from death or emigration. The subjects were between the ages of 27 and 30 when their criminal records were obtained from the Danish National Police Register. This register includes reference to the paragraph of Danish law violated and date of arrest for each offense resulting in contact with police for any citizen. Danish criminal record keeping is "probably the most comprehensive and accurate in the western world" (Wolfgang 1977, p. v). For purposes of this study, the following violations of the Danish Criminal Code were considered acts of violence: murder; rape; assault (specifically paragraphs referencing violence against authority, such as assaulting a police officer), bodily injury, violence, or threats of violence; and robbery with violence or threats of violence. Criminal records were found for 10,918 (38 percent) of the 28,879 subjects. Violent offenders numbered 735; these were 6.7 percent of offenders and 2.5 percent of the entire cohort.

Reliance on official records of police contact overlooks the many crimes that are not detected by police, resulting in less-than-perfect measurement of violent behavior. Nevertheless, research into the relation between official and self-reported sources of criminality data suggests that official records may be used for an operational definition of the "trait" of underlying criminality in individuals (although not all of their individual crimes) (Erickson et al. 1972). If bias does occur, it is that the hidden criminal tends to be less serious and recidivistic (Christie et al. 1965; Hindelang et al. 1979).

Results

Types of violent offenses. Percentages of subjects committing each of five types of violent offenses, as a function of total number of violent offenses committed, are shown in Table 1. Assault and robbery accounted for the majority of violent acts. All individuals who had been arrested three or more times for violent behavior had at least one arrest for a charge of assault. Rapists were few, and the proportion of violent offenders who raped appeared to decrease with increasing recidivism.

Concentration of violent crime. Of the 735 violent offenders, 562 (76.5 percent) committed only a single violent offense. The remaining 24.5 percent were more active in violent offending. Table 2 presents percentages of subjects who had committed zero, one, two, three, or four or more violent offenses. In this way the total number of violent offenders is divided into subgroups defined by number of

Table 1. Percentage of one, two, and three or more time violent offenders responsible for each category of violence

Violent offense type	One time violent offenders (%) ($n = 562$)	Two time violent offenders (%) ($n = 126$)	Three or more time violent offenders (%) ($n = 47$)
Murder	0.7	3.2	0.0
Rape	3.7	2.4	2.0
Robbery	15.7	28.8	36.1
Aggravated assault	3.4	5.8	4.2
Assault	76.5	92.1	100.0

Note. Percentages sum to more than 100 because multiple violent offenders could be responsible for more than one type of violence. Reprinted with permission from Guttridge et al. (1983).

Table 2. Distribution of violent offenders and violent crimes

Offense history	No. of individuals ($n = 28,879$)	No. of violent offenses ($n = 993$)	% of cohort	% of offenders	% of violent offenders	% of violent offenses
Violent offenders						
Number of offenses						
1	562	562	1.95	5.15	76.50	56.60
2	126	252	0.44	1.15	17.10	25.40
3	24	72	0.08	0.22	3.36	7.20
4	23	107	0.08	0.21	3.10	10.80
Nonviolent offenders	10,183		35.26	93.27		
Nonoffenders	17,961		62.19			

Note. Reprinted with permission from Guttridge et al. (1983).

violent offenses committed. Also in Table 2 are the percentages of all violent offenses committed by the cohort for which each frequency subgroup was responsible. As indicated by the table, 43.4 percent of all the violent offenses were committed by the repeat violent offenders. These men comprised 23.6 percent of the violent offenders, 1.6 percent of the total offenders in the cohort, and only 0.6 percent of all the men in the cohort. The concentration of violent crime is greater in this cohort than the concentration for general crime (violent plus nonviolent). That is, 45 percent of the total crimes were committed by 6.1 percent of the cohort (not shown in Table 2), but 43.4 percent of the violent crimes (a similar proportion) were committed by 0.6 percent of the cohort.

This degree of concentration of violent offenses in the hands of a minuscule subgroup of subjects suggested the hypothesis that these repeatedly violent individuals may have "specialized" in violent criminal acts.

Specialization for violence. The issue of specialization is debated in the criminological literature. Much of the discrepancy in findings seems to stem from variation in the definitions of specialization used for research. For example, Wolfgang et al. (1972), who concluded that specialization did not exist in their Philadelphia birth cohort, defined specialization as consecutive commission of the same type of offense. This definition has merit, but is somewhat limited in that it would exclude a case history of 10 rapes alternating with 10 other crimes. We suggest an alternate definition:

> *Specialization in violence* has been observed if an individual who commits a violent offense is more likely to commit a subsequent violent offense than an individual who commits a nonviolent (property) offense.

This definition is currently used in many psychiatric settings. Studies have shown that the best predictor of violent inpatient behavior in a psychiatric hospital is prior arrest for violent behavior (Volavka 1987). Armed with this definition of specialization, we attempted to determine if specialization existed among the 173 repeat violent offenders in the birth cohort (the potential specialists).

We compared individuals with an initial violent offense to individuals with an initial property offense by computing the proportions of each of these groups who committed at least one subsequent violent offense. (The offense defined as "initial" for this analysis was not necessarily a subject's first offense of any kind.) Offenders with an initial violent offense had more prior offenses than did subjects with an initial property offense, so that it was necessary to control for this variable. Controlling (by statistical covariance) for the number of offenses prior to the initial offense and subsequent to that offense, a first-time violent offender was 1.94 times more likely to commit a violent act among his future offenses than was a first-time property offender. This effect was also found when analyses were restricted to offenses committed before the age of 18 years; this suggests that specialization for violence (as defined here) occurs in both juvenile and adult offenders (Guttridge et al. 1983).

Commission of other types of crimes by violent offenders.   Although they did seem to specialize in violence, the violent offenders had committed more of every type of crime than had other offenders in the cohort. Violent offenders averaged 7.76 total offenses, as opposed to an average of 2.61 total offenses for nonviolent offenders. Also, the repeat violent offenders had higher numbers of total offenses

Table 3.   Violent offending as a function of recidivism

No. of offenses	% of offenders committing at least one violent act
1	1.45
2	1.98
3	2.63
4	3.24
5	4.10
6	4.43
7	4.67
8	5.72
9	4.31
10	4.08
11	4.21
12	6.18
13	6.31
14	7.28
15	6.12
16	6.63
17	7.92
18	9.30
19	10.38
20	8.29

Note. Reprinted with permission from Guttridge et al. (1983).

than the one-time violent offenders. For example, one-time violent offenders had committed an average of 3.66 property offenses, two-time violent offenders averaged 5.50 property offenses, and three-time violent offenders averaged 8.65 property offenses (nonviolent offenders averaged .97 property offenses). Table 3 addresses the relation of violent offending to overall recidivism from another viewpoint. It illustrates that it becomes more likely that an individual will behave violently if he has committed many crimes. Only 2.63 percent of three-time offenders had committed violent acts. In contrast, about 10 percent of the men credited with 18 or more crimes had committed violence. (Nonetheless, even among these serious recidivists with 18 or more arrests, 90 percent did not engage in violence.)

Age at onset of criminal behavior.   Table 4 presents the mean number of crimes of violence in a criminal career as a function of offender's age at first arrest for any type of crime. As age at first arrest increases, the likelihood of violence during the criminal career decreases. Indeed, subjects first arrested before they were 16 years old are much more likely to engage in violence than subjects first arrested later on in life.

Age at commission of violent act.   In this cohort the prevalence of violence is age dependent. By age 15 to 16 years the rate of violence is 2.5 percent. It rises steeply to over 8 percent by age 18, and reaches 9 percent at age 25. After age 25 the rate of violence drops suddenly to 1 percent by age 28. The majority (70 percent) of violent offenses were committed when the offender was between the ages of 18 and 25 years. The peak age for violent offending, 20 years, is slightly later than the peak age for all offenses, 17 years.

Table 4.   Mean number of violent crimes committed in a criminal career as a function of age at first arrest

Age at first arrest	Mean no. of violent offenses in entire career
8–10	0.25
11–13	0.24
14–16	0.22
17–19	0.11
20–22	0.04
23–25	0.03

Note. Reprinted with permission from Guttridge et al. (1983).

Summary

Our investigation of the violent subjects in this cohort has demonstrated that men likely to commit violent crimes can be distinguished from other criminals. Men who become violent begin committing crimes at a very early age, and they typically commit many offenses over time before their first arrest for violence. They commit most of their violent acts when they are 18 to 25 years old. These men do seem to specialize in violence; nevertheless, they commit more than their share of all other types of crime as well. The violent offenders, 2.5 percent of the cohort, were responsible for 17 percent of the cohort's crime. Intervention aimed at these very few individuals, if successful, could yield a substantial reduction in the overall crime rate. But first, we must be able to discern the individuals to be targeted. This investigation pointed to several epidemiological descriptors that place individuals at risk for violence (age at onset, prior recidivism, and age). Yet it is still true that the majority of our subjects with these descriptors did not have records for violence. The very low base rates for violence in the population would cause most predictive efforts based on these epidemiological factors to be false positives. The search for predictors of violent behavior must continue in other areas.

CONGENITAL CORRELATES OF VIOLENCE

Our earlier investigation of violence in a Danish birth cohort provided evidence for specialization in violent offending, even among juvenile offenders. Specialization may begin even earlier than the first arrest. There is a large literature demonstrating that aggressive behavior is a consistent pattern in some males, beginning in very early childhood and continuing to develop into criminal violence in adulthood (Loeber and Dishion 1983; McCord 1983; McGee et al. 1984; Olweus 1979; Robins 1966). Together these findings suggest that some factors operating very early in human development may contribute to emergence of a persistent violent response style in certain individuals. Congenital factors operate at the beginnings of human development. These factors include inherited characteristics and perinatal (pregnancy, neonatal, and delivery) complications. We next describe studies from our research group addressing genetic and perinatal correlates of criminal violence. Note that these factors are in all cases determined many years before criminal violence is manifested. There are often 18 to 25 years of experience interposed between a predisposing congenital factor and the illegal violent behavior. The relationship between congenital factors and violent behavior, therefore, would require considerable strength to be detected through 20-odd years of intervening experiential "noise."

Genetic Factors

First we will consider the evidence for genetic influences on criminal violence. There have been three approaches to genetic studies in this area. Family studies have shown that the best family predictor of antisocial behavior in sons is criminal arrest in their fathers (Robins 1966). This relation has not been specifically studied for violent acts. Family studies are limited, however, by the fact that the father contributes a psychosocial environment as well as genes to his sons. Another method for detecting genetic influence involves the study of twins. Identical twins have identical genes; fraternal twins are as genetically similar as nontwin siblings. Since the twins are born at almost the same time and are almost always reared together, greater similarity of behavior within identical twin pairs than within fraternal twin pairs is attributed to their greater genetic similarity. A review by Mednick and Volavka (1980) notes that across a series of studies, identical twins have a greater concordance for criminal behavior than do fraternal twins. A definitive population study (Christiansen 1977) found 35 percent concordance for identical twins and 13 percent concordance for fraternal twins. Studies such as these have provided us with evidence for genetic influences on criminal involvement, but usually too few subjects have been included for analyses of violent crime. Moreover, assumptions about the twin method have been questioned. After all, identical twins are not only more similar genetically but are also treated more similarly by their family and friends. It is possible that their similar criminal behavior is in part due to this similar treatment.

Adoption Studies

To address this problem, adoption studies have been designed. These are natural experiments in which the effects of genetic and rearing influences may be separated to a relatively high degree. For example, if the biological son of a severely criminal father is adopted away at birth to a noncriminal family and that son becomes severely criminal, this may be seen as evidence (with appropriate controls) that the criminal father passed on to his son a biological characteristic that predisposed both men to criminal acts. Crowe (1975) found evidence of a relationship between criminal behavior in an adopted-away child and its biological mother. Similarly, Cadoret (1978) found that antisocial behavior in adoptees is significantly related to antisocial behavior in the biological parents.

In Denmark, we gathered a birth cohort of all 14,427 nonfamilial adoptions from 1924 to 1947. For each adoption we recorded the psychiatric hospital diagnoses and court conviction histories of the adoptee, the biological mother and father, and the adoptive mother and father. Court convictions were taken as an index of the individual's criminal involvement, and occupation was taken as an index of the individual's socioeconomic status (Svalastoga 1959).

Conviction rate. The conviction rates of the subjects whose conviction records could be completely identified are shown in Table 5. The rates for biological fathers and their adopted-away sons are considerably higher than those of adoptive fathers. The adoptive father rate (6.2 percent) is a little below the average rate in the population (8 percent) for men of the same age range and time period (Hurwitz and Christiansen 1971). Most of the criminal adoptive fathers were one-time offenders; male adoptees and their biological fathers were more heavily recidivistic. The conviction rates of the women in this study were lower than those of the men but followed the same pattern. In view of these negligible rates of conviction for women, the analyses will concentrate on male adoptees.

The size of the population permits segregation of subgroups of adoptees with combinations of convicted and nonconvicted biological and adoptive parents in a design analogous to the cross-fostering model used in behavior genetics. If neither the biological nor the adoptive parents are convicted, 13.5 percent of the sons are convicted. If the adoptive parents are convicted and the biological parents are not, this figure rises only to 14.7 percent. However, if the adoptive parents are not convicted, and the biological parents are, 20.0 pecent of the sons are convicted. If the adoptive parents as well as the

Table 5.   Conviction rates of completely identified members of adoptee families

Family member	No. identified	No. not identified	Conviction rate by number of convictions			
			0	1	2	>2
Male adoptees	6,129	571	0.841	0.088	0.029	0.049
Female adoptees	7,065	662	0.972	0.020	0.005	0.003
Adoptive fathers	13,918	509	0.938	0.046	0.008	0.008
Adoptive mothers	14,267	160	0.981	0.015	0.002	0.002
Biological fathers	10,604	3,823	0.714	0.129	0.056	0.102
Biological mothers	12,300	2,127	0.911	0.064	0.012	0.013

biological parents are convicted, 24.5 percent of the sons are convicted. These data favor the assumption of partial genetic etiology. Simply knowing that an adoptive parent has been convicted of a crime, however, does not reveal how criminogenic the adoptee's environment has been. At conception, on the other hand, the genetic influence of the father is complete. Thus this is not a fair comparison between environmental and genetic influences but indicates only that sons whose biological parents have court convictions for criminal offenses have an increased probability of becoming convicted.

The relation between criminal law convictions in the sons and degree of recidivism in the biological parents is positive and relatively linear (Figure 1). Note that the rate of convictions in the sons of biological parents with three or more offenses is twice that of the sons whose biological parents have no convictions.

The chronic offender.   The chronic offender is infrequent but commits a markedly higher proportion of crimes in a cohort. This high rate of offending suggested the hypothesis that genetic predisposition plays a substantial role in these most deviant cases. In one U.S. birth cohort study (Wolfgang et al. 1972), the chronic offender was defined as one who had been arrested five or more times; these chronic

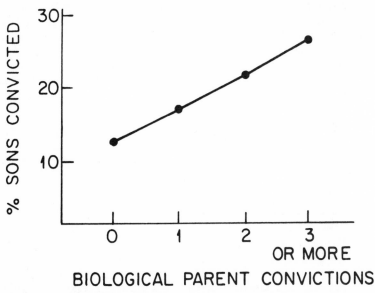

Figure 1.   Percentage of adoptive males convicted by biological parent convictions.

offenders who comprised 6 percent of the males had committed 52 percent of the offenses. In our adoption cohort, we recorded court convictions rather than arrest data. If we select as chronic offenders those with three or more court convictions, they were 4.1 percent of the male adoptees. This small group of recidivists accounts for 69.4 percent of all court convictions for all the male adoptees, a high concentration of crime in a small fraction of the cohort.

Figure 2 depicts the strong relationship between chronic offending in biological parents and chronic offending in their sons. The mean number of convictions for the chronic adoptee increases sharply as a function of biological parent recidivism. Note, however, that a genetic influence is not sufficient to produce criminal convictions in the adoptee. Of those adoptees whose biological parents have three or more convictions, 75 percent never received a court conviction.

Degree of genetic relatedness.   There are instances where a biological mother, or a biological father, or both, contributed more than one child to this population. Most of these children, who were full- or

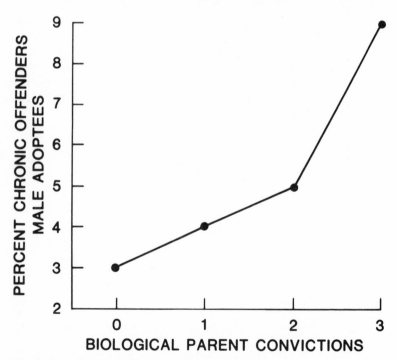

Figure 2.   Chronic offending in the male adoptees.

half-siblings, were placed in different adoptive homes. The probability of any one male adoptee being convicted is 0.159; the probability of at least one of a pair of unrelated, separated male adoptees being convicted is 0.293. The probability of both of a pair being convicted is 0.025. Thus the concordance rate for pairs of unrelated, separated male adoptees is 8.5 percent. This can be viewed as a baseline.

Table 6 shows that as the closeness of the genetic relationship increases (from unrelated to half-siblings to full-siblings), the concordance for criminal convictions increases. Note that the half-siblings and full-siblings with convicted biological fathers have a concordance rate of 30.8 percent.

The results suggest that a number of these separated adoptee siblings inherited some common characteristic that made both of them vulnerable to criminal behavior. In those instances in which the biological father is criminal, the effect is enhanced. Given the validity of the heritable effect for crime discussed thus far, does it extend to violent offending in particular?

Property versus violent offenses.   Figure 3 presents the adoptees convictions separated into property and violent convictions. Those categorized as property offenders had no convictions for violent offenses. Those categorized as violent offenders may have also committed property offenses. Note that there is a definite relationship between biological parent and adopted-away son for property convictions; but there is no significant relationship for violent offenses.

These results are completely congruent with a large Swedish adoption study (Cloninger and Gottesman 1987), which also found that property crime was under genetic influence and violent crime was not. These negative findings intrigued us, especially in light of an

Table 6. Concordance for criminal law convictions in male adoptees (unrelated and biological siblings) placed in separate adoptive homes

Degree of genetic relationship	% pairwise concordance
Unrelated, reared apart	8.5
Half-siblings, reared apart	12.9
Full-siblings, reared apart	20.0
Half- and full-siblings, reared apart; criminal father	30.8
Unrelated "siblings" reared together in adoptive home	8.5

exception to them that surfaced recently. Moffitt (in press) examined the influence of a biological parent's psychiatric diagnosis on the violent crime of the adoptee. If one biological parent was a chronic criminal and the other had a "social problem" psychiatric diagnosis (e.g., drug or alcohol addiction, personality disorder), the offspring registered almost a threefold increase in the proportion of convicted violent offenders over the remainder of the population. Of course, parent couples with this unfortunate combination of chronic crime and mental illness were few (4.3 percent of the cohort), but their adopted-away sons were twice as likely as the sons of nondeviant biological parents to be repeat offenders, to be convicted before age 19, and to be imprisoned for more than 6 months.

This may represent a distinct genetic contribution from the psychiatrically ill mother or may simply reflect the especially wretched pregnancy and nonoptimal fetal development experienced by adoptees with addicted, mentally disordered, or antisocial mothers. We are continuing to explore this finding at the present time.

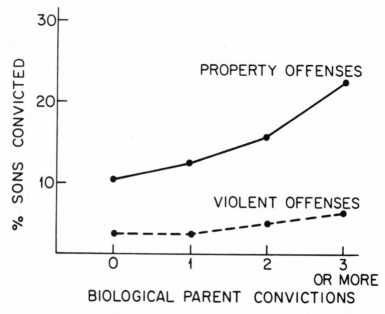

Figure 3.   Percentage of male adoptee property offenders and violent offenders by biological parent convictions.

Perinatal Factors

This leads us directly to the second of the congenital factors possibly contributing to violent behavior, perinatal problems. Several studies have demonstrated a relation between perinatal factors and criminal behavior. In 1971, Litt studied perinatal disturbances in a birth cohort of 1,944 consecutive births in Rigshospitalet in Denmark between January 1, 1936, and September 30, 1938. He found that perinatal trauma predicted impulsive criminal law offenses. Lewis et al. (1979) compared a group of aggressive, incarcerated delinquents with less aggressive, nonincarcerated delinquents. They concluded that the seriously delinquent children were significantly more likely to have sustained perinatal trauma than the nonincarcerated delinquent children. Similarly, Mungas (1983) found that in a group of psychiatric patients, perinatal factors were significantly related to violence. Wolff et al. (1982) found that the number of minor neuropathological signs (soft signs) was negatively correlated with age of onset of delinquency, especially among boys who had committed crimes of violence. These neuropathological signs are "generally interpreted as nonspecific behavioral markers of subclinical neurological deficit and they have been related etiologically to poor obstetrical or pediatric care, infantile undernutrition and the like" (Wolff et al. 1982, p. 274).

Assessment issues. The assessment of perinatal problems presents certain difficulties. Although delivery difficulties may be observed by a competent on-site rater, other pregnancy problems can be extremely elusive. A pregnant woman might indulge in an inappropriate diet, might ingest drugs and alcohol, or might subject herself (and her fetus) to other detrimental environmental conditions. If those conditions are not so severe that they result in gross fetal malformations, they might never come to the attention of the researcher.

Minor physical anomalies. The difficult-to-detect pregnancy problems discussed above can lead to the death or serious malformation of the fetus. But pregnancy complications may also produce less severe disturbances in the development of the fetus. For example, let us consider the development of the ears. The ears begin low on the neck of the fetus and slowly drift into their accustomed positions. With the introduction of some teratogenic event or substance, the development may be slowed or stopped and the ears' drift upward will terminate prematurely, resulting in low-seated ears. Such a minor malformation is an example of disturbed fetal development and is termed a minor physical anomaly (MPA) (Smith 1970). It is reasonable to assume that the teratogenic agents that cause such visible physical anomalies at a specific time during fetal development also produce covert anomalies in concurrently developing organs or organ systems, including the central nervous system. Thus a count of such apparent anomalies may be seen as an index of hidden anomalies (including possible central nervous system damage). While some heritability of MPAs has been demonstrated, Rapoport et al. (1974) and Waldrop and Halvorsen (1971) noted that MPAs are strongly associated with disorders of pregnancy (e.g., rubella during pregnancy or bleeding during the first trimester).

MPAs and hyperactivity.   MPAs are strongly related to hyperactivity. Waldrop et al. (1978) found that the newborn count of MPAs explains almost half of the variance in hyperactivity at age 3. In addition, Fogel et al. (1985) found support for a relationship between hyperactivity in males and MPAs. Hyperactivity in boys is, in turn, highly related to later serious delinquency (Satterfield 1987).

MPAs and criminal behavior.   In the context of a prospective study, we examined the relation of MPAs to police records of criminal law offenses. The MPAs were assessed in a sample of 129 boys (aged 12) by an experienced pediatric neurologist. Previous research by Waldrop and colleagues (1978) has shown that almost all of the MPAs detected at 12 years of age were present at birth. The sample of 129 boys was followed up in police records when the subjects were 21 years of age.

The results indicated that MPAs were totally unrelated to property offenses if the offender had no violent offenses on his record. MPAs were, however, strongly related to violent offending. (These violent offenders may have also had property offenses.) This was true when social class was controlled. More careful inspection of the data revealed that the MPAs predicted violence *only* for individuals reared in unstable, nonintact families. A stable family environment seems to compensate for the biological vulnerability represented by the MPAs (Mednick and Gabrielli 1983).

Perinatal-family stability interaction.   In another study, data were examined from a random sample of 847 children drawn from a Copenhagen birth cohort of 9,125 consecutive deliveries. Aggressiveness (e.g., bullying, fighting) was assessed at age 18 by the subjects' teachers. Children with many perinatal difficulties were judged to be at high risk. These children were compared to low-risk children. A similar interaction to the one noted above was found; perinatal difficulties predicted violence only for offenders who were raised in unstable environments (Baker and Mednick 1984).

This interaction between perinatal problems and family stability has been previously noted. In 1964, Drillien reported that premature babies do relatively poorly in school. Drillien noted that the long-term disadvantage for the premature infants was especially marked if the child was raised in an unstable, disturbed family setting. On the other hand, premature children raised in stable homes showed no or minimal disadvantage.

CONCLUSION

Genetic Factors

The data summarized support the conclusion that genetic factors predispose to crime. This predisposition is limited, however, to property crime. An exception illustrated by the Moffitt (in press) study suggests that if one biological parent is registered for crime and the other biological parent for personality disorder or substance abuse, the probability of violent offending is increased almost threefold in the son. However, because these mothers and fathers frequently provided less-than-ideal conditions for the developing fetus, the effect may be perinatal rather than genetic.

Perinatal Factors

Perinatal complications have not been widely studied in relation to criminal offending; perhaps this is because of the difficulties imposed by assessment and by the time span between the birth and subsequent violence (approximately 20 years). However, two studies that found indices of perinatal problems to relate to later violence rather than to property crime were briefly described. These findings are highly consonant with repeated reports of a high incidence of brain dysfunction in violent offenders (Nachshon and Denno 1987). Stable family rearing seems able to compensate for the perinatal damage.

The findings reviewed here suggest the conclusion that obstetrical complications may subtly compromise brain function, reducing the ability of some individuals to inhibit violent impulses. The consequent long-standing violent response style ultimately culminates in violent criminal offending. Some years ago, Helen Erskine (personal communication) collated epidemiological data showing very strong relations between level of obstetrical health of populations and levels of violent offending. Erskine pointed out that these correlations were subject to many interpretations. The demonstration of this relation within the context of a prospective study (with social class controlled) supports the view that obstetrical complications may be directly implicated in adult violence.

The level of obstetrical care in many areas and subpopulations in the United States is atrocious, especially in relation to our national wealth. Perhaps it will require the threat of further societal violence to motivate the improved obstetrical care that would give our neonates the use of a more adequate share of their inherited potential.

REFERENCES

Baker RL, Mednick SA: Influences on Human Development: A Longitudinal Perspective. Boston, Kluwer-Nijhoff Publishing, 1984

Cadoret RJ: Psychopathology in adopted-away offspring of biologic parents with antisocial behavior. Arch Gen Psychiatry 35:176–184, 1978

Christiansen KO: A review of studies of criminality among twins, in Biosocial Bases of Criminal Behavior. Edited by Mednick SA, Christiansen KO. New York, Gardner Press, 1977, pp 45–88

Christie N, Andenaes J, Skerbaekk S: A study of self-reported crime. Scandinavian Studies in Criminology 1:86–116, 1965

Cloninger CR, Gottesman II: Genetic and environmental factors in antisocial behavior disorders, in The Causes of Crime: New Biological Approaches. Edited by Mednick SA, Moffitt TE, Stack SA. Cambridge, UK, Cambridge University Press, 1987, pp 92–109

Crowe R: An adoptive study of psychopathy: preliminary results from arrest records and psychiatric hospital records, in Genetic Research in Psychiatry. Edited by Fieve R, Rosenthal D, Brill H. Baltimore, Johns Hopkins University Press, 1975

Drillien CM: The Growth and Development of the Premature by Birth Infant. Baltimore, Williams & Wilkins, 1964

Erickson ML: The changing relationship between official and self-reported measures of delinquency: an exploratory predictive study. Journal of Criminal Law, Criminology, and Political Science 63:338–395, 1972

Fogel CA, Mednick SA, Michelsen N: Hyperactive behavior and minor physical anomalies. Acta Psychiatr Scand 72:551–556, 1985

Guttridge P, Gabrielli WF, Mednick SA, et al: Criminal violence in a birth cohort, in Prospective Studies of Crime and Delinquency. Edited by Van Dusen KT, Mednick SA. Boston, Kluwer-Nijhoff Publishing, 1983

Hindelang MJ, Hirschi T, Weiss JG: Correlates of delinquency: the illusion of discrepancy between self-report and official measures. American Sociological Review 42:571–587, 1979

Hurwitz S, Christiansen KO: Kriminologi. Copenhagen, Gyldendal, 1971

Lewis DO, Shanok SS, Balla DA: Perinatal difficulties, head and face trauma, and child abuse in the medical histories of seriously delinquent children. Am J Psychiatry 136:419–423, 1979

Litt SM: Perinatal complications and criminality. Doctoral dissertation, University of Michigan, 1971

Loeber R, Dishion T: Early predictors of male delinquency: a review. Psychol Bull 94:68–99, 1983

McCord J: A longitudinal study of aggression and antisocial behavior, in Prospective Studies of Crime and Delinquency. Edited by Van Dusen KT, Mednick SA. Boston, Kluwer-Nijhoff Publishing, 1983

McGee R, Silva PA, Williams S: Perinatal, neurological, environmental and developmental characteristics of seven-year-old children with stable behavior problems. J Child Psychol Psychiatry 25:573–586, 1984

Mednick SA, Gabrielli WF: Biological, psychological, and sociofamilial factors in crime. (Final report, grant #81-IJ-CX-009.) Washington, DC, National Institute of Justice, 1983

Mednick SA, Volavka J: Biology and crime, in Crime and Justice: An Annual Review of Research, Vol 2. Edited by Morris N, Tonry M. Chicago, University of Chicago Press, 1980

Moffitt TE: Parental mental disorder and offspring criminal behavior: an adoption study. Psychiatry, Interpersonal and Biological Processes (in press)

Mungas D: An empirical analysis of specific syndromes of violent behavior. J Nerv Ment Dis 171:354–361, 1983

Nachshon I, Denno D: Violent behavior and cerebral hemisphere dysfunctions, in The Causes of Crime: New Biological Approaches. Edited by Mednick SA, Moffitt TE, Stack SA. Cambridge, UK, Cambridge University Press, 1987

Olweus D: Stability of aggressive reaction patterns in males: a review. Psychol Bull 86:852–875, 1979

Rapoport JL, Quin PO, Lamprecht F: Minor physical anomalies and plasma dopamine-g-hydroxylase activity in hyperactive boys. Am J Psychiatry 131:387–390, 1974

Robins LN: Deviant Children Grown Up. Baltimore, Williams & Wilkins, 1966

Satterfield H: Childhood diagnostic and neurophysiological predictors of teenage arrest rates: an eight-year prospective study, in The Causes of Crime: New Biological Approaches. Edited by Mednick SA, Moffitt TE, Stack SA. Cambridge, UK, Cambridge University Press, 1987

Smith D: Recognizable Patterns of Human Malformation. Philadelphia, WB Saunders, 1970

Svalastoga K: Prestige, Class, and Mobility. Copenhagen, Gyldendal, 1959

Volavka J: Electroencephalogram among criminals, in The Causes of Crime: New Biological Approaches. Edited by Mednick SA, Moffitt TE, Stack SA. Cambridge, UK, Cambridge University Press, 1987

Waldrop MF, Halvorsen C: Minor physical anomalies and hyperactive behavior in young children. Exceptional Infant 2:343–380, 1971

Waldrop MF, Bell RA, McLaughlin B, et al: Newborn minor physical anomalies predict short attention span, peer aggression, and impulsivity at age three. Science 199:563–564, 1987

Witkin HA, Mednick SA, Schulsinger F, et al: Criminality, aggression, and intelligence among XYY and XXY men. Science 193:547–555, 1976

Wolff PH, Waber D, Bauemeister M, et al: The neuropsychological status of adolescent delinquent boys. J Child Psychol Psychiatry 23:267–279, 1982

Wolfgang ME: Foreword, in Biosocial Bases of Criminal Behavior. Edited by Mednick SA, Christiansen KO. New York, Gardner Press, 1977

Wolfgang ME, Figlio RM, Sellin T: Delinquency in a Birth Cohort. Chicago, The University of Chicago Press, 1972

Chapter 3

Prediction of Assaultive Behavior in Psychiatric Inpatients: Is It Possible?

Antonio Convit, M.D.
Judith Jaeger, Ph.D.
Shang Pin Lin, Ph.D.
Morris Meisner, Ph.D.
Jan Volavka, M.D., Ph.D.

Chapter 3

Prediction of Assaultive Behavior in Psychiatric Inpatients: Is It Possible?

V iolence by psychiatric patients is of considerable concern. It would be desirable to predict which patients are likely to become assaultive. Accurate prediction would enable clinicians to design strategies to prevent the violent behavior from developing. Clinicians have been "vastly overrated as predictors of violence" (Monahan 1984, p. 10). Research has shown that clinicians are more likely to be wrong than right when making a long-term prediction of whether a person will be violent. An accuracy of one in every three predictions has also been reported by investigators doing multiyear follow-up studies of patients who had been committed for dangerousness and then released by the courts (Cocozza and Steadman 1974; Steadman 1972, 1977; Steadman and Cocozza 1974; Thornberry and Jacoby 1979). Although poor accuracy in long-term clininical prediction of dangerousness has been clearly demonstrated, clinicians are still expected in their everyday work to make dangerousness risk assessments.

Monahan (1981) provided an exhaustive critical analysis of violence prediction research, calling for greater methodological rigor. Predictions of violence and dangerousness have a poor record, in part for the following reasons:

1. The predictions are generally made on the basis of clinical judgment. No systematic method is utilized. Clinicians make a predictive decision based on what they feel about the case. This feeling is generally based on a combination of clinical and behavioral information about the patients.
2. No uniform definition of violence is used in research on violence prediction. Thus comparison between different studies may yield

apparent inconsistencies. For example, some researchers use the term *assault* to define the behavior being predicted, whereas others may use the term *dangerousness*. *Dangerousness* may be used to mean physical violence directed toward people, antisocial behavior such as stealing, agitated behavior such as throwing bottles in a public park, or any number of other behaviors. Also compounding the problems that arise from the lack of a clear definition of violence are problems with its method of detection. Frequently, the method of detection has low sensitivity and unknown reliability.

3. The prediction of violence is generally made for a different setting than the one in which the patient is observed. For example, it has been typical for clinicians to make predictions about the future behavior of a patient in the community based on the patient's behavior in an institution. Clinicians have based their predictions on observations of the patient's behavior in the structured, more predictable, and safe environment of the hospital and then have extrapolated these predictions to the community—a setting that is at times unsafe, unstructured, and less predictable than the institutional setting.

4. The prediction is usually made for too long a period of time. It has not been unusual for clinicians to attempt to predict behaviors for up to several years in the future.

5. Clinicians who make risk assessments (predictions) fail to take into account the base rate of the behavior in the setting for which it is being predicted. For example, where the base rate is 5 percent (i.e., 5 percent of all patients in a given setting actually become violent), there have been studies in which 30 percent of patients are labeled as "dangerous." This results in a large number of false positive predictions.

In response to this poor record, researchers have become more sophisticated. Monahan (1984) refers to a "second generation" of studies in violence prediction. In these more recent studies, actuarial methods of prediction are used (Klassen, in press; Steadman 1982), variables are collected in and/or pertain to the same environment for which the prediction is made (Klassen 1986), and predictions are made for a shorter period of time after evaluation (McNeil and Binder 1987; Werner et al. 1983). In some cases, the research design has included a cross-validation of the initial prediction method in a second patient sample (Steadman and Morrissey 1982). An accounting for the base rate of the behavior to be predicted has, however, not been incorporated into most prediction methods.

We have attempted to address some of the shortcomings of prior research that have contributed to the poor record. The complexities of conducting research on the predictive validity of dangerousness assessment are many. We have concentrated our efforts on the narrowly defined problem of predicting assaultiveness in psychiatric inpatients. By developing the methodology for this simpler problem, we hope to learn how to manage the methodologically more complex assessment of dangerousness on patients' discharge to the community. A description of the series of steps we used and the methodology we employed follows.

SUGGESTED STEPS ON HOW TO CARRY OUT PREDICTION RESEARCH

We have found the sequence outlined here to be useful in conducting research to predict assaultiveness, one aspect of violent behavior. We defined *assaultiveness* as physical contact including pushing, slapping, punching, scratching, kicking, and strangling.

Preparation Phase

1. Select, on the basis of original hypotheses and on the literature, a set of variables that may be considered potential predictors of assaultiveness. After a review of the literature, we chose 22 variables and tested them as potential predictors. Convit et al. (in press) provides a literature review. These 22 variables were either dichotomous (rated as present or absent) or continuous. The dichotomous variables were childhood enuresis, fire setting, cruelty to animals (Felthous and Kellert 1987; Hellman and Blackman 1966), victimization as a child, paternal and maternal deviance (heavy alcohol use, intravenous drug use, and psychiatric hospitalization), history of head trauma, subject's heavy drug or alcohol use, violent and nonviolent suicide attempts (Van Praag 1982), and self-reported arrests and convictions for violent and nonviolent crime.

A rating scale measuring the deviance of family environment was constructed from the following eight historical variables: mother's psychiatric hospitalization, alcohol use, and intravenous drug use; father's psychiatric hospitalization, alcohol use, and intravenous drug use; patient's physical abuse as a child; and family intactness. Each of these eight historical variables was coded as 0 (absent) or 1; the average of the sum thus obtained was used as a measure of deviance of family environment.

The biological variables measured included a neurological evaluation and an electroencephalogram (EEG). A quantified neurological rating scale was administered by either of two physicians who had no knowledge of the hypotheses being tested. These physicians could not be blind to group membership due to the risks of working with assaultive patients. The scale consisted of 66 items and included standard "hard signs" as well as several "soft signs" such as overflow, face-hand test, graphesthesia, and stereognosis. A score of 1 indicated abnormality; 0 indicated normality. The neurological abnormality score for any patient consisted of the sum of the item scores divided by the number of items tested. (See Appendix 1 for full scale.) The EEG was recorded using the 10–20 system. The EEG tracings were read by an observer who was blind to patients' assaultiveness history. The tracings were inspected for theta, delta, and sharp waves, discharges, lateralization, effect of hyperventilation, and presence of low voltage.

   2. *Identify a subset of variables that are associated with assaultiveness that are likely to confound the results and use them for matching or stratification.*   Several demographic variables have been shown to be associated with violence. Age (Craig 1972; Reid et al. 1985), sex (Reid et al. 1985; Tardiff and Koenigsberg 1985; Tardiff and Sweillam 1980), and psychiatric diagnosis (Craig 1972; Tardiff and Sweillam 1982) have been described as being related to violence in psychiatric patients. We chose to examine a second or higher order set of predictors potentially associated with violence. Thus we considered age, sex, race, chronicity of illness, and psychiatric diagnosis to be potentially confounding factors. These variables were therefore used as matching variables for the selection of control subjects.

Case-Control Study Phase

Subjects were inpatients selected from a 1,300-bed, state psychiatric facility (Manhattan Psychiatric Center) located in a large metropolitan area serving predominantly indigent inner-city patients.

   1. *Identify patients who are clearly assaultive.*   The 69 violent patients in this study were selected from a group of 87 consecutive transfers to a special 15-bed unit specifically designed for the management of violent behavior. Eighteen violent patients were excluded because they had diagnoses of mental retardation or seizure disorder. See Table 1 for a demographic description of the patients and Table 2 for a comparison of the violent patients to the overall hospital population.

   To qualify for transfer to this ward and, consequently, to be subjects in our study, patients had to exhibit at least two instances of assaultive behavior in the preceding month and to have been unmanageable on their home wards. In general, patients treated on this ward were the most violent patients in the hospital. All violent patients in this study had been hospitalized for at least 1 month prior to entering the special ward (with the exception of one patient who was transferred to the violent ward 10 days after admission to the hospital). The majority of patients had been hospitalized longer than 6 months prior to transfer.

2. *Identify patients who are clearly not assaultive. From this group select a subset of controls by matching on selected variables.* The 40 controls were selected from other wards of the same hospital. They had committed no serious violent acts, and they had been hospitalized for at least 6 months. The control sample was selected so that the distributions for age, sex, race, and chronicity of illness were as close as possible to those of the 69 violent patients. There were no significant differences in the distributions. By matching for these variables, we would isolate other variables that we were interested in

Table 1. Demographic description of patient set

	Nonviolent subjects		Violent subjects		Non-CBD violent subjects	
No. of patients	40		87		69	
Average age						
years	31.9		31.1		31.3	
range	18–49		17–52		18–52	
Average age at 1st psychiatric hospitalization						
years	20.38		16.8		18.9	
range	8–45		3–35		6–45	
Sex						
Male	32	(80%)	63	(72%)	51	(74%)
Female	8	(20%)	24	(28%)	18	(26%)
Race						
White	9	(23%)	22	(25%)	13	(19%)
Nonwhite	31	(77%)	65	(75%)	56	(81%)
Diagnosis						
Schizophrenia	34		55		50	
Mental retardation	0		10		0	
Bipolar illness	6		14		12	
Personality disorder	0		8		7	

Note. CBD = coarse brain disease; differences between either violent group and the controls were not significant.

testing as potential predictors. Diagnoses of all patients were established by consensus of two psychiatrists using DSM-III (American Psychiatric Association 1980) criteria. We were unable to locate patients with the diagnosis of personality disorder who had not been violent for entry into the control group.

3. *Use the potential predictors of interest to discriminate between the assaultive patients and the matched controls.* Violent and nonviolent patient groups were compared on the dependent variables using the chi-square test for categorical variables, and the *t*-test, analysis of variance, (ANOVA), or analysis of covariance (ANCOVA) for con-

Table 2. Comparison of the violent patient group to the total hospital population averaged from the beginning and the end of the study period

	Total hospital population (Average of 10/1/83 + 5/1/85)	Violent subjects
No. of patients	1,254	87
Average age		
years	42.6	31.1*
range	17–94	17–52
Average age at first psychiatric hospitalization		
years	not assessed	16.8
range		3–35
Sex (%)		
Male	64.9	72.4
Female	35.1	27.6
Race (%)		
White	29.2	25.3
Nonwhite	70.8	74.7
Diagnosis (%)		
Schizophrenia	71.8	63.2
Mental retardation	1.4	11.5
Bipolar illness	4.1	16.1
Personality disorder	0.6	9.2
Other	22.0	0

Note. The violent patients are included in the total hospital figures.
*$p<.001$.

tinuous variables. Those analyses that involved variables obviously affected by the presence of coarse brain disease (CBD) (such as neurological abnormality score and EEG) were performed separately on a subset of violent patients from which 18 patients who had CBD were excluded (10 patients with mental retardation, 7 with seizure disorder, and 1 with hemiparesis secondary to a stroke sustained in childhood).

Findings on historical variables. A self-reported history of violent crime was the strongest historical discriminator between the violent patients and their matched controls, with a higher prevalence of violent crime among violent patients ($\chi^2 = 13.81$, 1 df, $p = .0002$ for arrests; $\chi^2 = 9.40$, 1 df, $p = .0004$ for convictions). Nonviolent crime did not distinguish between the groups. Violent patients also tended to have a mother with a history of psychiatric hospitalization ($\chi^2 = 3.22$, 1 df, $p = .07$) and to have attempted violent suicide ($\chi^2 = 3.22$, 1 df, $p = .07$) more frequently than nonviolent patients. Nonviolent suicide attempts did not distinguish the two groups (Table 3).

Drug or alcohol history did not differ between groups. A history of head trauma, enuresis, fire setting, or cruelty to animals failed to distinguish violent from nonviolent patients. Heavy alcohol use in

Table 3. Comparisons of violent and nonviolent groups for historical variables

Variable	Nonviolent controls ($n=40$) (%)	Violent total group (CBD + Non-CBD) ($n=87$) (%)
Arrests for nonviolent crimes	50.0	45.9
Convictions for nonviolent crimes	17.5	23.5
Arrests for violent crimes	7.5	42.4**
Convictions for violent crimes	5.0	31.8**
Nonviolent suicide attempts	16.7	22.5
Violent suicide attempts	19.4	38.3*
Mother psychiatric hospitalization	7.7	23.3*
Deviance of family environment	0.18	0.2+

Note. CBD = coarse brain disease.
*$p < .08$ by χ^2 test.
**$p < .002$ by χ^2 test.
+$p < .05$ by t-test. See text for definition of deviance.

the father and physical abuse as a child tended to be more prevalent among violent patients; however, these differences failed to reach statistical significance.

The mean (± SD) score on the family environment deviance rating scale was significantly greater for violent (0.27 ± 0.25) than for nonviolent (0.18 ± 0.15) patients (t = 2.12, 124 df, p = .013). *Findings on biological variables.* To test the relationship between neurological status and violence in "functional" mental disorders, we repeated the analyses for the neurological variables and EEG excluding the 18 violent patients with evidence of CBD.

Non-CBD violent patients had a significantly higher abnormality score on the neurological scale than did controls (ANOVA, F = 7.56, 1/108 df, p < .01) even after neuroleptic dose was taken into account (ANCOVA, F = 3.12, 2/101 df, p < .05). No single brain area differentiated the violent from the nonviolent group. There were no significant group differences on any of the EEG variables. From these results we selected four risk factors, or predictors, to be used in the development of the actuarial prediction model: history of convictions for violent crime (C), history of violent suicide attempts (S), neurological abnormality score (N), and, deviance of family environment (F).

Development of the Actuarial Model Using the Predictors Selected

1. Choose an appropriate statistical model. The particular statistical model chosen depends on the type of predictors used (categorical, continuous, or both). We chose a statistical model to create a linear expression with the predictors, as identified in the case-control study, as terms. This linear expression is then used actuarially to make the prediction. The four risk factors that emerged from the univariate analyses described above were investigated with multivariate analyses, and a linear model was derived. We used *conditional* logistic regression and did not use discriminant analysis (although the four risk factors separated the violent patients from the controls significantly when discriminant analysis was used) because this method allowed us to reintroduce the possible effect of age, which had been controlled for in selecting the nonviolent patients.

Logistic regression analysis (Kleinbaum et al. 1982) was used to develop a model relating odds (likelihood) of violent inpatient behavior among young male schizophrenics to the four risk factors. The model expresses the logarithm of the odds of a given inpatient's violent behavior as a weighted linear sum of the individual patient's risk factors with the weights being the estimated regression coefficients (β_i). The exponential of the coefficients, that is, exp (β_1), can be interpreted as indicating the change in odds of inpatient violence associated with every unit change in the corresponding risk factor in the regression model. This yielded a linear equation of the form

$$\text{Odds Ratio} = \exp(\beta_1 C + \beta_2 S + \beta_3 N + \beta_4 F)$$

where $\beta_1 \ldots \beta_4$ are the estimated regression coefficients and C, S, N, and F are the four risk factors. The sample utilized to obtain the coefficients was stratified into age groups (18 to 21, 22 to 25, 26 to 29, and 30 to 35) and a conditional logistic regression model was used. With the use of conditional logistic regression, the odds estimate is not an absolute one, but instead represents the odds of being violent relative to that for a designated baseline state. The baseline state is defined as the situation where all four risk factors have a value of zero. An odds ratio of inpatient violent behavior was computed from the fitted model for each patient relative to the baseline rate.

2. *Test power of the prediction equation by applying it retrospectively to a subgroup of case-control study subjects.* Most of the serious violence in our institution is committed by young schizophrenic males. Therefore, we restricted the original case-control sample in the following way: Only patients who were male, schizophrenic, and younger than 36 years of age were used to generate the regression equation. There were 51 patients (31 violent and 20 nonviolent) in this final sample.

The odds ratio obtained for each patient in this group of young schizophrenic patients could be used to assess the utility of the prediction equation to discriminate between violent patients and controls in the case-control study. This was done by rank ordering the patients by odds ratios, and then, on the assumption that the higher odds ratios would be found among the 31 violent patients, splitting the 51-patient sample into two sets: those ranked 1 to 31 and those ranked 32 to 51. Those ranked from 1 to 31 were predicted (or perhaps better said, postdicted) to be violent and those patients with ranks 32 to 51 were postdicted to be nonviolent. The nosologic sensitivity and specificity, the global value, and the diagnostic sensitivity and specificity of the method were determined (Table 4) and used to evaluate the usefulness of odds ratios in classifying violent and nonviolent patients. These analyses are routinely used to evaluate newly introduced screening tests (Feinstein 1985).

The nosological sensitivity of this new "test" for violence is the proportion of all the violent patients in the population studied that are detected by the test to be violent. The nosological specificity of the method is the proportion of the nonviolent patients in the population that are detected by the test to be nonviolent. The global value of the test is the proportion of all the violent and nonviolent patients in the population that are correctly detected by the test. The diagnostic sensitivity (also known as the value of positive result) represents the proportion of patients who are known to be violent out of those who are classified as such by the test. The diagnostic specificity (also known as the value of negative result) represents the proportion of patients who are known to be nonviolent out of those who were classified as such by the test. The proportion of patients correctly classified depends in part on the prevalence of violence in the population under study. Therefore, the diagnostic sensitivity and specificity are corrected for the prevalence of violence in the population by using the Bayes theorem (Feinstein 1985).

No prediction was involved in the case-control study; the term *postdiction* describes the classification of patients at the time when the outcome is known. The postdiction was significantly better than chance ($\chi^2 = 5.96, p < .02$). This ability of the equation to classify the patients in the case-control study is shown in Table 5.

Development of an Algorithm That Will Enable Prospective Classification of Patients as Assaultive or Nonassaultive

A prediction, by definition, is made before the outcome is known. The problem we faced was how to determine a priori a cutoff value for the odds ratio that could be used prospectively to separate the

Table 4. Hypothetical data in a diagnostic marker study

Observed	Test results	
	Positive	Negative
Diseased group	TP	FN
Control group	FP	TN

Where:

Nosological sensitivity	= TP/(TP + FN)	TP	= True Positive
Nosological specificity	= TN/(TN + FP)	FP	= False Positive
Global value	= (TP + TN)/N	TN	= True Negative
Diagnostic sensitivity	= TP/(TP + FP)	FN	= False Negative
Diagnostic specificity	= TN/(TN + FN)	N	= Number of subjects

subjects to be predicted as assaultive from those to be predicted as nonassaultive.

For the dichotomous prediction of assaultiveness from the odds ratio, one needs to determine in advance the appropriate cutoff point separating violent and nonviolent subjects in the distribution of these ratios. We used the distribution of ratios obtained in the case-control study, estimated that for a population of newly admitted young schizophrenic males the 3-month prevalence of assaultiveness would be 30 percent, and selected a diagnostic specificity of 50 percent. That diagnostic specificity indicates that the results would have no more than one false positive for every true positive classification. Using the Bayes theorem (Feinstein 1985), we computed the cutoff odds ratio and predicted that all patients with odds ratios above that cutoff would be assaultive. (Details of the computation are available on request.) The results of this computation are shown in Table 6.

Cross-Validate the Prediction Equation in a New Patient Sample

1. Identify newly admitted patients. In the same hospital used for the case-control study, we located within the first week after their

Table 5.   Postdicted and observed violence in case-control study

Observed	Postdicted		Total
	Yes	No	
Yes	23	8	31
No	8	12	20
Total	31	20	51

$\chi^2 = 5.96\ p < .02$
Nosological sensitivity = 74%
Nosological specificity = 60%
Global value   = 69%
Diagnostic sensitivity = 74% (not corrected for prevalence)
             = 44% (based on a hypothetical prevalence of 0.3)
Diagnostic specificity = 60% (not corrected for prevalence)
             = 84% (based on a hypothetical prevalence of 0.3)

admission 79 male patients younger than 36 years of age with the admission diagnosis of schizophrenia. These patients were not necessarily consecutive admissions; the rate of patients' identification and testing was determined primarily by the human resources available at that time. We do not believe that this method of patients' selection introduced a systematic bias.

2. *Measure each patient's individual values for the four risk factors, introduce them into the prediction equation, and compute a total.* Within the first week after admission of these 79 patients, a physician who was not aware of the experimental design administered the predictor test battery. The battery consisted of our quantified neurological examination, a questionnaire on deviancy of family environment (see above for details concerning these instruments), a history of conviction for violent crimes, and a history of violent suicide attempts. The results of this battery were then used to compute each patient's odds ratio for violent behavior.

3. *Classify patients according to the predictions equation.* At Manhattan Psychiatric Center, 80 percent of newly admitted male patients' violent incidents that occur in the first 6 months of hospitalization actually occur in the first 3 months (unpublished data). The mean

Table 6. Diagnostic specificity as a function of odds ratio and prevalence (abridged table)

		Prevalence					
Odds Ratio		0.25	0.26	.	0.30	.	0.35
	1.00	0.28	0.29	.	0.33	.	0.39
	1.44	0.29	0.31	.	0.35	.	0.40
	.	.	.	.	.	.	.
	8.45	0.42	0.43	.	0.49	.	0.54
	8.82	0.42	0.44	.	<u>0.50</u>	.	0.54
	.	.	.	.	.	.	.
	618.08	0.90	0.91	.	0.91	.	0.94

Note. Cells in the table represent diagnostic specificity. The underscored cell indicated that for prevalence of assaultive behavior of 30 percent if one used 8.82 as the cutoff odds ratio there will be at least one true positive for every false positive classification.

duration of stay is 3 months. We, therefore, decided to assess the efficacy of our predictive model by studying the behavior of the patients during their first 3 months of hospitalization. Estimating the 3-month incidence of assault in newly admitted patients to be 30 percent (the value of 30 percent was arrived at in a pilot study) and selecting a diagnostic specificity of 0.5 (or 50 percent), the cutoff odds ratio was determined to be 8.45 (Table 6). All patients with odds ratios above 8.45 were thus predicted to be assaultive and those with odds ratios of 8.45 or less were predicted to be nonassaultive.

  4. Follow the patients for a predetermined period of time and record their assaultive behavior. Actual assaultiveness was determined on the basis of behavioral data collected during the first 3 months of the patients' hospital stay or up until discharge (whichever came first). These data were collected by three research associates who were not aware of the patients' odds ratios or the nature of the study design. Patients were classified as violent if they were found to have committed at least one physical assault during the period studied. A physical assault was defined as actual physical contact such as hitting, kicking, pushing, biting, hair pulling, scratching, or strangling. Patients involved in a fight in which they were reported not to hit back were not judged to be assaultive during the fight. The three research associates went to each patient's ward and reviewed the change of shift reports (ward journal), the patient's chart progress notes, and the medication record for prn medication (i.e., that which is administered at the discretion of ward staff in response to agitated behavior). Any entries pertaining to violent behavior for that patient in that weekly period were recorded verbatim. These abstracted records were then analyzed to determine which incidents met the criteria for physical assault as defined above.

  The interrater reliability of the determination of patients' in-hospital assaultiveness was then assessed. To accomplish this, each of the three raters independently reviewed records for the first month of hospitalization of 31 patients, obtained the verbatim statements, and then determined the number of times that each patient had been assaultive in that period (the date and time of day were recorded for each event).

  Interrater reliability for the judgment of whether a recorded incident met our criteria for an assault was high; the intraclass correlation coefficient (ICC) (Bartko and Carpenter 1976) was .95. There were 18 patient-month periods during which all three raters found no assaults; there were 15 assaults that all three raters agreed on; and there were two events classified as physical assault by only two raters. The discrepancies were both in patients who had had more than 2 assaults coded for that month, so the disagreement did not affect the patient's classification as violent or nonviolent.

If a patient committed at least one physical assault on another person, he or she was classified as violent for the purpose of this project. If no such record was found, the patient was classified as nonviolent.

5. *Compare the prediction with the outcome.*   Table 7 displays the results of the prediction. Of 79 subjects, 52 were classified correctly. This finding was significantly different than chance ($\chi^2 = 4.21$, $p < .05$). To get a clearer idea of what our results mean, they have to be contrasted with the results of other researchers in the field. Table 8 displays such a comparison. Our prediction study is the only one in the published literature (1) that is a cross-validation, (2) that uses an actuarial method of prediction utilizing few predictors (making it cost-effective), and (3) that has been shown to be moderately accurate in an intermediate period of follow-up (3 months).

Table 7.   Predicted and observed violence in the prospective study within three months of follow-up after admission

Observed	Predicted		Total
	Yes	No	
Yes	11	8	19
No	19	41	60
Total	30	49	79

$\chi^2 = 4.21$ $p < .05$
Nosological sensitivity = 58%
Nosological specificity = 68%
Global value   = 66%
Diagnostic sensitivity   = 37% (not corrected for prevalence)
                         = 46% (based on a hypothetical prevalence of 0.3)
Diagnostic specificity   = 84% (not corrected for prevalence)
                         = 78% (based on a hypothetical prevalence of 0.3)

Table 8. Comparison of studies predicting hospital assaultiveness

Study	Prediction method	Length of follow-up	Cross validation	NSS %	NSP %	GV %	PREV %	DSS %	DSP %
Convit/Volavka (Case-control Study)	Actuarial	N/A	No	74	60	69	61	74	60
Convit/Volavka (Prospective)	Actuarial	90 days	Yes	58	68	66	32	46	78
Steadman/Morrissey Indicted (1982)	Actuarial	Var. (avg. 18 months)	No	34	81	63	39	54	66
Steadman/Morrissey Unindicted (1982)	Actuarial	Var. (avg. 18 months)	Yes	42	66	59	30	35	73
Steadman/Morrissey Involuntary (1982)	Actuarial	Var. (avg. 18 months)	Yes	36	75	72	7	10	94
Werner/Yesavage Postdiction (1983)	Clinical	7 days	No	42	71	63	30	38	74
McNeil/Binder (1987)	Clinical	3 days	No	28	93	62	16	42	87

Note. NSS = nosologic sensitivity
NSP = nosologic specificity
GV   = global value
PREV = prevalence
DSS = diagnostic sensitivity
DSP = diagnostic specificity
N/A = not applicable

SUGGESTIONS FOR FUTURE RESEARCH

Study Other Risk Factors

The actuarial method we have developed for predicting which patients are likely to become assaultive while hospitalized can be improved by incorporating other risk factors and by decreasing the time period for which the prediction is made. Potential risk factors other than those we have used have been described in the literature. Assaultive and fear-inducing behavior immediately preceding the psychiatric admission have been found to predict violent behavior in the hospital (Rossi et al. 1986). Patients emergently committed because they were judged as dangerous to others were more frequently assaultive during the first 72 hours after admission than those emergently committed for other reasons (McNeil and Binder 1987). A relationship between psychopathology, as measured by the Brief Psychiatric Rating Scale (BPRS), and assaultive behavior has been described (Tanke and Yesavage 1985; Yesavage 1983a, 1983b).

The schizophrenic subtype may be an important determinant. Krakowski et al. (1986) reported that different subtypes of schizophrenics have different temporal patterns of in-hospital assaultiveness. They reported that when paranoid schizophrenics become assaultive, they do so within the first week of hospitalization. Undifferentiated schizophrenics tend to assault later. Personality diagnoses have been associated with certain types of violence. Hare (1983) has shown that a significant proportion of prison inmates can be labeled psychopaths or sociopathic personality disorders according to DSM-III criteria. His psychopathy inventory, although not validated in psychiatric populations, may yield a reasonable measure of psychopathy in psychiatric populations as well. Psychopathy is a trait clinically observed in many assaultive patients and deserves exploration.

Environmental factors are likely to be important in the development of assaultive behavior in at least a subgroup of patients. Violence on psychiatric wards has been found to fluctuate by hour of day (Depp 1983). Depp explained these variations by stating that they correspond to periods of increased activity demanded of patients following periods of inactivity.

During the 1960s and early 1970s, several researchers explored what they called "interaction distance" and "body buffer zone." Interaction distance was defined as the space that persons establish between themselves and others. Aggressive hospital patients were reported to utilize greater interaction distances than did normals (Horowitz 1965). The body buffer zone was defined as that area around a person within which anxiety is produced when another person enters. Larger body buffer zones have been reported in schizophrenics compared to nonschizophrenics (Hall 1966; Horowitz et al. 1964). In a double-blind study, prison inmates with histories of aggression had significantly larger body buffer zones than did nonaggressive inmates (Hildreth et al. 1971). From the results of these studies, one can hypothesize that the level of crowding on psychiatric wards would probably affect the number of assaults displayed.

Some environmental factors that could also be associated with aggression are temperature, time from last meal and consequent level of hypoglycemia (Mednick and Volavka 1980), and presence of other assaultive patients on the ward. Environmental factors are poorly understood, mostly because they have not been rigorously studied. The little that is known about environmental concomitants or precipitants of inpatient violence probably reflects the large methodological problems encountered in their study.

Shorten the Time for Which the Prediction Is Made

When a psychiatrist evaluates a patient for the first time, a tentative diagnosis is made on the basis of that interview. On observing the patient's behavior over time, the initial diagnostic impression is confirmed or revised. In an analogous fashion, one could make a short-term prediction (e.g., 2 weeks) based on the first cross-sectional evaluation of the patient and a revised second prediction by adding variables that reflect the patient's behavior in the first 2 weeks of hospitalization. Conceptually, the first prediction would be based mostly on trait variables such as family and personal history, neurological score, and level of sociopathy. The second prediction would then add state-dependent variables such as environmental factors, BPRS scores, violence in the first 2 weeks, and so forth.

Another suggestion for future work on the prediction of assault is that investigators could focus their evaluations on patients who assault repeatedly. We have conducted our work on violence at two state institutions: one in a large urban area, the other in a rural setting. All the data reported up to this point in the chapter were collected at Manhattan Psychiatric Center, which is in a large urban area. At both of these institutions we have observed the existence of a small group of patients who assault repeatedly and are responsible for the majority of the assaults. Approximately 5 percent of the patients assault more than once during their hospital stay. This small group is responsible for more than 50 percent of all the assaults in the hospital. It is apparent then that this group of repeat assaulters deserves special attention. Future research should focus on the repeat assaulters by contrasting them with those patients who assault only once. This approach may yield a new set of risk factors that could then be used to develop a predictive model for this recidivistic group. This type of approach both uses a control group (those who assault once), which makes good intuitive sense and is probably more cost-effective, and would allow testing of interventions to be carried out.

In this chapter we have shown that the development of methodology to predict assaultiveness is clearly possible. There are several points to bear in mind in adapting some of this methodology to prediction of dangerousness on release. As Mulvey and Lidz (1985) have elegantly pointed out: first, the outcome variable must be appropriately chosen. One must make sure that the behavior being predicted actually is the same that is being measured by the outcome variable. For example, if the prediction is of "dangerous" behavior, it is possible that most of the violent behavior committed by the individuals who are predicted to be dangerous goes unnoticed if one looks only at arrest history. Second, the prediction method must be reliable. The reliability of the method will set the upper limit on the validity of the method. To make a method reliable, it must be done actuarially with operationalized procedures. Third, dangerousness must not be equated with commitment. The recent work of McNeil and Binder (1987) has dealt with this issue.

The next step we are taking in our research efforts is to develop a methodology to study environmental factors and how they affect assaultiveness. Once we have a better understanding of how situational/environmental factors interact with the patients' propensity toward violence in the hospital, we will be in a position to expand our efforts to prediction of violence in the community.

REFERENCES

American Psychiatric Association: Diagnostic and Statistical Manual of Mental Disorders, 3rd ed (DSM-III). Washington, DC, American Psychiatric Association, 1980

Bartko JJ, Carpenter WT: On the methods and theory of reliability. J Nerv Ment Dis 163:307–317, 1976

Cocozza J, Steadman H: Some refinements in the measurement and prediction of dangerous behavior. Am J Psychiatry 131:1012–1020, 1974

Convit A, Jaeger J, Lin SP, et al: Prediction of violence in psychiatric patients, in Biological Contributions to Crime Causation. Edited by Moffitt T, Mednick S. Amsterdam, Martinus Nijhof, 1987

Craig TJ: An epidemiologic study of problems associated with violence among psychiatric inpatients. Am J Psychiatry 139:1262–1266, 1972

Depp FC: Assaults in a public mental hospital, in Assaults Within Psychiatric Facilities. Edited by Lion JR, Reid WH. New York, Grune & Stratton, 1983

Feinstein AR: Clinical epidemiology, in The Architecture of Clinical Research. Edited by Feinstein AR. Philadelphia, WB Saunders Co, 1985, pp 414–453

Felthous AR, Kellert SR: Childhood cruelty to animals and later aggression against people: a review. Am J Psychiatry 144:710–717, 1987

Hall ET: The Hidden Dimension. New York, Doubleday & Co, 1966

Hare RD: Diagnosis of antisocial personality disorder in two prison populations. Am J Psychiatry 140:887–890, 1983

Hellman DS, Blackman N: Enuresis, firesetting and cruelty to animals: a triad predictive of adult crime. Am J Psychiatry 122:1431–1435, 1966

Hildreth AM, Derogatis LR, McKusker K: Body buffer zone and violence: a reassessment and confirmation. Am J Psychiatry 127:1641–1645, 1971

Horowitz M: Human spatial behavior. Am J Psychother 19:20–28, 1965

Horowitz M, Duff D, Stratton L: The body buffer zone: an exploration of personal space. Arch Gen Psychiatry 11:651–656, 1964

Kleinbaum DG, Kupper LL, Morgenstein H: Epidemiologic Research Principles and Quantitative Methods. Belmont, Calif, Lifetime Learning Publications, Wadsworth, 1982

Krakowski M, Volavka J, Brizer D: Psychopathology and violence: a review of literature. Compr Psychiatry 27:131–148, 1986

McNeil DE, Binder RL: Predictive validity judgments of dangerousness in emergency civil commitment. Am J Psychiatry 144:197–200, 1987

Mednick S, Volavka J: Biology and crime, in Crime and Justice. Edited by Morris N, Tonry M. Chicago, University of Chicago Press, 1980

Monahan J: Predicting Violent Behavior: An Assessment of Clinical Techniques, Vol 114. Beverly Hills, Calif, Sage Publications, 1981

Monahan J: The predictive of violent behavior: toward a second generation of theory and policy. Am J Psychiatry 141:10–15, 1984

Mulvey EP, Lidz CW: Back to basics: a critical analysis of dangerousness research in a new legal environment. Law and Human Behavior 9:209–219, 1985

Reid WH, Bollinger MF, Edward G: Assaults in hospitals. Bull Am Acad Psychiatry Law 1–4, 1985

Rossi AM, Jacobs M, Monteleone M, et al: Characteristics of psychiatric patients who engage in assaultive or other fear-inducing behaviors. J Nerv Ment Dis 174:154–160, 1986

Steadman HJ: The psychiatrist as a conservative agent of social control. Social Problems 20:263–271, 1972

Steadman HJ: A new look at recidivism among Patuxent inmates. Bull Am Acad Psychiatry Law 5:200–209, 1977

Steadman H, Cocozza J: Careers of the Criminally Insane. Lexington, Mass, Lexington Books, 1974

Steadman HJ, Morrissey JP: Predicting violent behavior: a note on a cross-validation study. Social Forces 61:475–483, 1982

Tanke ED, Yesavage JA: Characteristics of assaultive patients who do and do not provide visible clues of potential violence. Am J Psychiatry 142:1409–1413, 1985

Tardiff K, Koenigsberg HW: Assaultive behavior among psychiatric outpatients. Am J Psychiatry 142:960–963, 1985

Tardiff K, Sweillam A: Assault, suicide, and mental illness. Arch Gen Psychiatry 37:164–169, 1980

Tardiff K, Sweillam A: Assaultive behavior among chronic inpatients. Am J Psychiatry 139:212–215, 1982

Thornberry T, Jacoby J: The Criminally Insane: A Community Follow-Up of Mentally Ill Offenders. Chicago, University of Chicago Press, 1979

Van Praag HM: Depression, suicide and metabolism of serotonin in the brain. J Affective Disord 4:275–290, 1982

Werner PD, Rose TL, Yesavage JA: Reliability, accuracy, and decision-making strategy in clinical prediction of imminent dangerousness. J Consult Clin Psychol 51:815–825, 1983

Yesavage JA: Bipolar illness: correlates of dangerous inpatient behavior. Br J Psychiatry 143:554–557, 1983a

Yesavage JA: Inpatient violence and the schizoprenic patient. Acta Psychiatr Scand 67:353–357, 1983b

Appendix 1   Neurologic Scale (Antonio Convit, M.D., The Nathan S. Kline Institute for Psychiatric Research)

Name of Patient _____ Date of Hospital Admission _____

Patient ID _____ Date of Test ____/____/____ (Month/Day/Year)
       (5-10)   (11-16)

Current Neuroleptic _____ Daily Dose _____ Cogentin Current Daily Dose _____
                  (17-18)   (19-22)   (23-24)

Handedness: Comb ____ Write ____ Throw ____ Brush ____ Hole ____ Telescope ____ Step on Roach ____
L = 1, R = 2   (37)   (38)   (39)   (40)   (41)   (42)   (43)

R-L Orientation: Right Hand ____ Left Hand ____ Right Hand to Right Ear ____
0 = Correct   (44)   (45)   (46)
1 = Incorrect

              Left Hand to Left Ear ____ Right Hand to Left Ear ____
                         (47)   (48)

              Left Hand to Right Ear ____ Identify Right and Left on Examiner ____
                         (49)   (50)

Pupillary Reaction: ____ **Nystagmus:** ____ **Extra Ocular Movements:** ____
0 = Normal   (51)   0 = Absent   (52)   0 = Normal   (53)
1 = Abnormal   1 = Suggestive   1 = Abnormal
                      2 = Present

Visual Field: Single Stimulation ____ Double Stimulation ____
0 = Normal   (54)   (55)
1 = Abnormal

Facial Asymmetry: ____ **Hearing:** Rinne ____ Weber ____
0 = Absent   (56)   0 = Normal   (57)   (58)
1 = Present   1 = Abnormal

Tongue Asymmetry: ____ **Rombergs:** ____
0 = No   (59)   0 = Normal   (60)
1 = Yes   1 = Abnormal

Appendix 1 Neurologic Scale (*continued*)

Hopping: Right _____ Left _____
(61) (62)
0 = Normal
1 = Abnormal

Standing Balance: _____ Walking: _____
(63) 0 = Normal (64)
0 = Normal 1 = Abnormal
1 = Abnormal

Walking Associated Asymmetry: _____ Muscle Strength Asymmetry: _____
(65) (66)
0 = Normal 0 = Normal
1 = Abnormal 1 = Abnormal

Arm Drift Present: _____
(68)
0 = No
1 = Yes

Finger to Nose: Eyes Open Right _____ Eyes Open Left _____
(69) (70)
0 = Normal Eyes Closed Right _____ Eyes Closed Left _____
1 = Suggestive (71) (72)
2 = Abnormal

Finger Thumb Opposition: One Hand Right _____ One Hand Left _____
(73) (74)
0 = Normal Overflow Right _____ Overflow Left _____
1 = Suggestive (75) (76)
2 = Yes Two Hands Right _____ Two Hands Left _____
(77) (78)

Appendix 1 Neurologic Scale (*continued*)

Card No. _____
    (1–2)

Pronation-Supination: One Hand Right _____ Overflow Right _____
0 = Normal   (3)   (4)
1 = Suggestive   One Hand Left _____ Overflow Left _____
2 = Abnormal   (5)   (6)

                 Two Hands Right _____ Two Hands Left _____
                        (7)   (8)

Foot Taps: One Foot Right _____ Overflow Right _____
0 = Normal   (9)   (10)
1 = Suggestive   One Foot Left _____ Overflow Left _____
2 = Abnormal   (11)   (12)

                Two Feet Right _____ Two Feet Left _____
                     (13)   (14)

Heel to Shin: Right _____ Left _____ Tandem Gait: _____
0 = Normal   (15)   (16)   0 = Normal   (17)
1 = Abnormal   1 = Abnormal

Tendon Reflex Asymmetry: _____ Tendon Reflexes Amplitude: _____
0 = No   (18)   0 = (+1) or (+2)   (19)
1 = Yes   1 = Areflexia
                              2 = Hyperreflexia

Appendix 1 Neurologic Scale (*continued*)

Clonus: Right _____ Left _____
                (20)   (21)
0 = No
1 = Yes

Plantar Response (Babinski): Right _____ Left _____
                                    (22)   (23)
0 = No
1 = Yes

Face Hand Test: RF – LH _____ LF – RH _____ F – F _____ H – H _____
                         (24)   (25)   (26)   (27)
0 = Correct
1 = Extinguishes Left
2 = Extinguishes Right
3 = Irrelevant Answer

Graphesthesia: 3 Right _____ 8 Left _____ 1 Right _____ 7 Left _____
                       (28)   (29)   (30)   (31)
0 = Correct
1 = Incorrect

               8 Right _____ 1 Left _____ 7 Right _____ 1 Left _____
                       (32)   (33)   (34)   (35)

Astereognosis: Right Key _____ Quarter Left _____ Penny Right _____ Comb Left _____
                         (36)   (37)   (38)   (39)
0 = Correct
1 = Incorrect
               Key Left _____ Quarter Right _____ Penny Left _____ Comb Right _____
                        (40)   (41)   (42)   (43)

Appendix 1　Neurologic Scale (*continued*)

*Fist – Ring:　Left Arm Imitate ‗‗‗‗ (44)　Left Arm Continue ‗‗‗‗ (45)
0 = Normal
1 = Suggestive
2 = Abnormal/ Right Arm Imitate ‗‗‗‗ (46)　Right Arm Continue ‗‗‗‗ (47)

*Fist – Edge – Palm:　Left Imitate ‗‗‗‗ (48)　Left Continue ‗‗‗‗ (49)
0 = Normal
1 = Suggestive
2 = Abnormal　Right Imitate ‗‗‗‗ (50)　Right Continue ‗‗‗‗ (51)

*Fist – Stretch:　Left Imitate ‗‗‗‗ (52)　Left Continue ‗‗‗‗ (53)
0 = Normal
1 = Suggestive
2 = Abnormal　Right Imitate ‗‗‗‗ (54)　Right Continue ‗‗‗‗ (55)

*Items not used in studies reported on in this chapter.

Chapter 4

Clinical and Historical Correlates of Dangerous Inpatient Behavior

Jerome A. Yesavage, M.D.
David A. Brizer, M.D.

Chapter 4

Clinical and Historical Correlates of Dangerous Inpatient Behavior

The current skepticism regarding the ability of psychiatrists to predict violence may not be wholly justified. Although much of the research up until now on violence prediction has been hampered by illusory correlations and methodological flaws (Monahan 1981), these flaws are amenable to correction. Research in the prediction of violence may lend itself to state-of-the-art psychiatric research technology (Monahan 1984). Indeed, a "second generation" (Monahan 1984) of research based on short-term prediction, statistical approaches, and quantified outcome measures warrants optimism.

This chapter will describe studies from a program of research designed to identify significant correlates of inpatient violence. Findings relevant to each correlate will be described in turn. These studies were performed over several years on several hundred patients. This allowed us to perform multivariate analyses and to assess the relative importance of predictor variables in some of our later studies. We were also able to look at related questions, such as how clinicians use variables for predicting violence, and how this affects the accuracy of their predictions. These studies, taken as a whole, suggest that there are identifiable, quantifiable factors that are useful in the short-term prediction of violence by hospitalized patients with schizophrenia and other psychiatric diagnoses.

All studies were conducted on the Psychiatric Intensive Care Unit of the Veterans Administration Medical Center, Palo Alto, California. This 20-bed unit receives all acute admissions to the Veterans Administration Medical Center. Studies described in this chapter were conducted between 1977 and 1985.

A review of previous studies associated with inpatient violence

(Baron 1972; Kermani 1981; Lion 1972; Lion et al. 1974; Monahan 1981) indicated that the most important correlates of violence in our patients were likely to be severity of psychotic symptoms, low neuroleptic blood levels, severity of violent behavior preceding admission, military combat experience, and severity of childhood discipline. Our own preliminary studies, as described below, confirmed that a number of these variables were, in fact, correlated with violent acts in hospitalized schizophrenic patients.

A modified version of a scale developed by Lion (Student and Lion 1978) was used in all studies to record the number of days in which each patient was involved in a danger-related behavior (assault against others, verbal assault, and seclusion or restraint episodes). The number of days on which each event occurred at least once during the first 8 days of hospitalization was computed. These ratings had an interrater reliability of .73 by intraclass correlation on total score; reliabilities of all individual items were greater than .60 (Yesavage 1983a).

MAJOR CORRELATES OF INPATIENT VIOLENCE

Severity of Psychosis

In a study of 26 males (mean age 31 years, 25 with various subtypes of schizophrenic disorder, 1 with bipolar illness) consecutively admitted on 72-hour holds, significant correlations (alpha = .05 or less) were observed between admission scores on the Brief Psychiatric Rating Scale (BPRS) and patients' ratings over 8 days on the modified Lion scale (Yesavage et al. 1981).

The BPRS is an 18-item psychopathology rating scale that has been used in numerous psychiatric studies and has been shown to be a reliable measure of differences between patient groups (Overall and Klett 1972). The items segregate into the five factor scores commonly reported in BPRS data analyses: anxiety-depression, disorientation, thought disorder ("schizophrenia"), hostility-suspiciousness ("paranoia"), and emotional withdrawal-retardation factors. Scores on a thought disorder factor and on a thought disorder relative to depression factor, both derived from the BPRS (Overall and Klett 1972), as well as total BPRS scores were positively and significantly correlated with assaults against others and with verbal assaults. Ratings on the hallucinatory behavior, conceptual disorganization, and unusual thought content items were found to significantly predict both assaults against others and total number of assault-related behaviors. Additional BPRS scales such as excitement, grandiosity, and anxiety were significantly associated with the total number of assault-related events recorded for a patient, but not with the number of actual assaults in which each patient was involved. Lack of significant correlations between the BPRS hostility scale and assaultiveness measures lent support to previous studies (Blackburn 1968a, 1968b; Megargee 1971) showing that violent outbursts may erupt in individuals who display low overt hostility.

A subsequent study (Yesavage et al. 1982b) using an expanded sample of 79 involuntarily admitted patients (70 percent of whom had diagnoses of schizophrenia or schizoaffective disorder) replicated the previous finding of significant associations between certain BPRS scores and inpatient violent behavior (Table 1). Patients with at least one assaultive event during the first 8 days of hospitalization scored significantly higher on total BPRS score and on the excitement, unusual thought content, motor retardation, grandiosity, suspiciousness, mannerisms, and tension scales. It is of interest that, unlike in the previous study, assaultive patients had significantly higher ratings ($p < .001$) on the hostility scale than did patients without assaultive behavior. (This may be explained by the increased power resulting from the expanded sample size in the latter study.)

A third study (Yesavage 1983d) involved 207 consecutively involuntarily admitted male schizophrenics—according to DSM-III (American Psychiatric Association 1980) criteria—with a mean ($\pm$ SD) age of 33.8 ± 11.2 years. In this study, there were significant positive correlations between scores on two BPRS factors and all danger-related measures (Table 2). Five BPRS factors were identified from among the 18 scale scores by a type of factor analysis known as principal components analysis (Kim 1975). This kind of analysis can isolate underlying factors among the many scale scores that may be heavily intercorrelated. The BPRS factors significantly correlated with the danger-related measures were the schizophrenia factor (comprised of BPRS conceptual disorganization, hallucinations, and unusual thought content scales) and the paranoia factor (suspiciousness, hostility, and uncooperativeness scales).

Similar results were observed in a sample of 40 consecutively admitted male patients with DSM-III bipolar affective disorder (Yesavage 1983a). For these subjects, the BPRS psychosis (but not the paranoia) factor score was significantly correlated with both physical assaults and total number of danger-related events.

Low Neuroleptic Blood Levels

The finding of a direct correlation between core schizophrenic symptomatology and inpatient danger-related events led to asking how neuroleptic medications may control such symptoms and potentially violent acts. Since a number of previous studies (Jacobsson et al. 1976a, 1976b; Yesavage et al. 1982a) had demonstrated a correlation between serum thiothixene levels and reduction of schizophrenic symptomatology, it seemed reasonable to test the hypothesis that neuroleptic levels correlated with inpatient danger-related events in a schizophrenic population.

Neuroleptic serum levels were measured by fluorescent spectro-

Table 1. BPRS scores for patients with and without at least one assault-related event during their first 8 days of hospitalization

	Ward behavior (mean ± SD)	
BPRS Scale	Patients with one or more assaultive events ($n = 47$)	Patients with no assaultive events ($n = 32$)
Somatic concern	3.04 ± 1.33	2.33 ± 0.96
Anxiety[a]	3.89 ± 1.07	3.20 ± 1.10
Conceptual disorganization[b]	3.04 ± 1.26	3.40 ± 1.43
Guilt	2.65 ± 1.52	2.68 ± 1.44
Tension[a]	4.06 ± 1.18	3.46 ± 1.39
Mannerisms[a]	3.00 ± 1.65	2.28 ± 1.33
Grandiosity[b]	3.91 ± 1.71	2.84 ± 1.74
Depressive mood	2.61 ± 1.39	3.21 ± 1.47
Hostility[c]	4.36 ± 1.34	3.09 ± 1.53
Suspiciousness[a]	3.98 ± 1.42	3.25 ± 1.39
Hallucinations	3.82 ± 1.89	3.15 ± 1.67
Motor retardation[b]	1.82 ± 1.07	2.65 ± 1.34
Uncooperativeness	3.42 ± 1.19	3.15 ± 1.50
Unusual thought content[b]	4.27 ± 1.44	3.31 ± 1.67
Blunted affect	2.68 ± 1.35	3.12 ± 1.26
Excitement[c]	3.85 ± 1.74	2.40 ± 1.47
Disorientation	1.74 ± 1.42	1.58 ± 1.11
Total score[b]	60.42 ± 11.79	51.93 ± 9.70

[a] Patients who had one or more assaultive events had a significantly ($p < .05$) higher score on this item.
[b] Patients who had one or more assaultive events had a significantly ($p < .01$) different score on this item.
[c] Patients who had one or more assaultive events had a significantly ($p < .001$) higher score on this item.

Table 2. Correlation of BPRS factors and inpatient danger-related measures for 207 inpatients

BPRS factors	Inpatient danger-related measures				
	Physical assaults	Seclusion	Restraint	Verbal assaults	Total assaults
Schizophrenia	0.27**	0.48***	0.42***	0.47***	0.58***
Blunted affect	−0.21*	0.08	−0.10	−0.12	−0.11
Paranoia	0.20**	0.22**	0.18*	0.25**	0.26**
Depression or anxiety	−0.11	−0.15	0.00	−0.12	−0.05
Confusion	0.01	−0.10	−0.12	0.16	0.03

Note. $*p < .05$; $**p < .01$; $***p < .001$ (two-tailed).

metry on single test doses of 20 mg of thiothixene administered orally to 58 male DSM-III schizophrenic inpatients (Yesavage 1982). The acute single test dose method is strongly correlated ($r = .85$, $p < .001$) with steady state blood levels ($n = 15$). Significant ($p < .005$) negative correlations were found between serum levels of thiothixene and three of four measures of danger-related events (physical assaults, $-.48$; verbal assaults, $-.37$; assaults and other acts, $-.65$) during the first 8 days of subjects' hospitalization. Eight of the nine patients who were assaultive had serum levels that were below the group mean (13.3 ng/ml). The significance of these findings is that some schizophrenic patients with low neuroleptic blood levels may become violent because their core schizophrenic symptoms are not being adequately controlled with medication.

Act Leading to Admission

An additional correlate of physical assaults in the series of 40 male bipolar patients mentioned above (Yesavage 1983a) was the act leading to admission. A scale developed by Rabiner (personal communication) was used to rate the severity of violence of the act leading to admission. This 9-point scale is based on the report of the patient, the family, and that of peace officers and mental health professionals involved in the admission. Interrater reliability on this scale was calculated for 28 subjects rated by each of two raters. An intraclass correlation of .96 was obtained by using Bartko's (1966) two-way analysis of variance (ANOVA). The product-moment correlation between physical assaults during the first 8 days of hospitalization and violence preceding admission was .31 ($p < .05$).

Military Combat Experience

Although there may have been as many as 25,000 schizophrenic veterans who once served in Vietnam (Lawson et al. 1984), few studies have been made of this population. Given the association of Vietnam posttraumatic stress reaction with violence, it was decided to study the effect of veterans' Vietnam experience on their schizophrenic illness.

Measures of dangerousness were recorded during the first 8 days of hospitalization (as in our previous studies) for 80 consecutively admitted male Vietnam-era male patients with DSM-III diagnoses of schizophrenia (Yesavage 1983b). Of these subjects, 30 had been in Vietnam; of these, 20 had been in combat; 50 subjects had been neither in combat nor in Vietnam. Predictor variables for inpatient dangerousness included subjects' responses to a 7-item questionnaire that listed a number of experiences that a soldier might have had in

Vietnam. The best predictor of total inpatient danger-related events (verbal and physical assaults plus seclusion or restraint episodes) was the variable of whether the subject had been in combat in Vietnam. A factor (derived by principal component analysis from the questionnaire) relating to having seen killings and/or having killed someone during military service in Vietnam contributed additional information to the prediction of verbal and physical assault on the ward.

A second study (Yesavage 1983c) in this same patient population was then undertaken to determine the impact of criminal history vs. Vietnam combat experience on inpatient violent behavior. Seventy consecutively admitted male Vietnam-era schizophrenics (DSM-III) were studied. Of these, 27 subjects had been in Vietnam, 19 had been in combat, and 43 were neither in Vietnam nor in combat. Reliability of subjects' self-reported criminal activity both before and after military service was examined in 15 subjects in relation to arrest records. Fourteen of 15 subjects were truthful about their arrest record.

Criminality before service significantly correlated with Vietnam combat ($.42, p < .005$), criminality after the service ($.44, p < .005$), and inpatient assault ($.28, p < .05$). Vietnam combat experience significantly correlated with inpatient assault ($.31, p < .01$). Correlation between combat and criminality after the service was not significant ($-.13$).

To tease apart the independent influence of combat experience on inpatient assaults, stepwise multiple regression analyses were performed. In the first multiple regression analysis, the independent variables entered on the first step were criminality before and after the service; combat in Vietnam was then entered into the regression equation on the second step. This analysis was performed to determine whether Vietnam combat added anything over and above criminality to the model of prediction of inpatient assault based on criminality alone.

Vietnam combat significantly improved the overall regression equation ($F = 4.65$, 1/67 df, $p < .05$). When the analysis was performed in the opposite order, that is, with Vietnam combat entered on the first step followed by criminality before and after military service on the second, neither criminality variable significantly improved the overall regression equation (both F values were less than 1). These results confirmed the hypothesis that, in our population of male schizophrenics, violent behavior on the ward is better explained by subjects' war experiences than by their preadmission criminal behavior.

Childhood Discipline

Childhood discipline was found to be significantly correlated with inpatient assaults in both manic and schizophrenic populations at our hospital.

Principal component analysis was done on a Family Discipline Questionnaire (designed to measure the type and severity of discipline the patient had received as a child), which was administered to 85 of 100 consecutively admitted schizophrenic or schizoaffective patients (Yesavage et al. 1983). Subjects were asked to recall if they had been disciplined at various levels of severity (e.g., verbal discipline, spanking, beating, or punishment resulting in serious injury) by each of their parents.

Family discipline factors were found by multiple regression analysis to be associated with all danger-related measures. The extent to which the father was reported to have engaged in severe and mild discipline was associated with the commission of physical assaults by the patient. In addition, the questionnaire factor reflecting the extremely severe discipline (such as burns, fractures, and other injury) was associated with the overall measure of danger-related events on the ward.

In the previously discussed study of 40 bipolar disorder patients (Yesavage 1983a), childhood discipline was significantly ($p < .01$) associated with physical assault in the hospital. Along with degree of psychosis, presence of mania, and degree of violence of the act leading to admission, severe childhood discipline was highly correlated with committing inpatient assaults.

OTHER POTENTIAL CORRELATES OF INPATIENT VIOLENCE

Race

It has been reported that violence is more common among minorities, including blacks (Bell 1980). For example, the nonwhite murder rate is said to be 8 to 15 times that of whites. Discussions with the staff at the Psychiatric Intensive Care Unit lead to the expectation that black inpatients would have higher violence scores than white inpatients (Lawson et al. 1984). Such an expectation may be associated with differential treatment decisions regarding black and white patients. For example, in a retrospective chart review of schizophrenic inpatients, Flaherty and Meagher (1980) found that blacks were given more prn medication and were more likely to receive seclusion and restraint despite the absence of racial differences in psychopathology in this sample. Blacks were disproportionately secluded in another study (Soloff and Turner 1982) of treatment practices on an inpatient unit.

To examine the frequency of violent acts among black and white inpatients, 117 consecutively admitted males (24 blacks and 93 whites) with varying diagnoses were studied (Lawson et al. 1984). Each subject received a fixed dose of a neuroleptic (80 mg/day of thiothixene). There was a trend for a higher proportion of black patients to be diagnosed as having paranoid schizophrenia versus affective disorder ($\chi^2 = 3.16, p < .10.$). No significant racial differences were noted on mean neuroleptic serum levels (drawn 2 hours after a 20-mg test dose) or on total BPRS scores. However, substantial and significant differences were noted in the patients' scores on the modified Lion scale. Significantly ($p < .0001$) lower total danger-related event scores were noted for black versus white patients. Analysis of individual items on the Lion scale showed that blacks had significantly ($p < .05$) fewer episodes of verbal abuse; there was no significant racial difference on physical assaults.

The possibility that violent black patients may have been selected out of the mental health system (and referred to the criminal justice system) should be considered in attempting to account for these exceptional findings. Other historical correlates of inpatient violence (military combat experience and history of childhood discipline) were not measured in this study and may have differed between black and white subjects.

Drug Abuse

A frequently reported correlate of violence has been a history of drug abuse. Tinklenberg and Woodrow (Buss 1961), for example, found that alcohol was the drug most likely to be associated with violent crimes in juvenile offenders.

We studied dangerous behaviors as correlates of a history of drug and alcohol use in 85 male schizophrenic inpatients (Yesavage and Zarcone) 1983). History of drug use was elicited in a structured interview using a 26-item questionnaire that included questions about which substances were used, the frequency of use, and how the subjects behaved when they had had too much alcohol or drug. Eight factors accounting for 76 percent of the variance on the original 26-item questionnaire were isolated by principal component analysis. To determine the relative importance of each factor in relation to dangerousness, a stepwise multiple regression was performed using dependent measures of dangerousness from the Lion scale.

A history of alcohol and drug abuse was significantly related to measures of dangerousness. An interesting finding was that different aspects of drug abuse history were related to different measures of dangerousness. While the best predictor of inpatient assault, for example, was the drug abuse factor relating to history of blackouts and assaultiveness while taking drugs and favoring phencyclidine (PCP) as a drug of abuse (multiple R^2 = .26; β-weight = .43), the use of seclusion or restraint was strongly related to experiences of becoming "loud" while on drugs or alcohol (multiple R^2 = .38; β-weight = .47).

Self-Destructive Behavior

The presumed relationship between hostility and self-destructiveness (Schneideman 1975) was tested by measuring such behavior in hospitalized schizophrenics (Yesavage 1983e). Eighty consecutively admitted male DSM-III schizophrenics were rated on the Buss-Durkee Inventory (Buss 1961), a self-report measure of different kinds of hostility. This scale, which contains 75 true-false items divided into seven subscales, attempts to categorize various kinds of overt and covert hostility and has been shown to distinguish violent from nonviolent alcoholics and prisoners (Mullen et al. 1978; Rosenbaum et al. 1981). The number of days during which self-destructive and other dangerous behavior occurred among subjects over the 8-day study period was recorded.

Self-destructive acts were significantly correlated with six of the seven Buss-Durkee subscales (Table 3). A principal component analysis of the seven subscales isolated an indirect hostility factor (loading heavily on the indirect and irritable scales) and a direct hostility factor (reflecting hostility expressed directly). The direct hostility factor was highly correlated with both suicidal acts and seclusion episodes. Total BPRS scores over the first week of hospitalization did not correlate beyond a chance level with either the self-destructiveness or Buss-Durkee measures.

A significant correlation was thus demonstrated between suicidal and self-destructive acts and measures of hostility and violence in this patient sample. However, the self-report hostility measure did not correlate with the observer-rated measure of danger-related events (the Lion scale). It is possible that the two scales are measuring substantially different phenomena.

RECENT STUDIES ON CORRELATES OF DANGEROUS INPATIENT BEHAVIOR

Subsequent to confirming correlations between the previously discussed independent variables and dangerous inpatient behavior, we undertook a comprehensive evaluation of our hospitalized schizophrenic population to determine the relative importance of each of these correlates (Yesavage 1984a). Three years of data collection involving several hundred subjects were required to accumulate sufficient subjects (rated on all variables) to perform a multivariate analysis comparing the relative importance of each variable.

Data were collected on 70 male DSM-III schizophrenics over a 3-year period. The mean age of the patients was 32 years; 80 percent were white, 11 percent were black, and 9 percent were Asian and other races. As in the previous studies, data were collected over the first 8 days of hospitalization and included ratings of dangerous behavior on the ward (modified Lion scale); thiothixene serum levels following single 20-mg test doses; BPRS factor scores obtained on admission; ratings on the scale devised by Rabiner to measure the severity of violence of the act leading to admission; responses to questions concerning the type and severity of discipline the patient had received as a child; and a summary score of patients' responses to eight yes/no questions regarding their combat experience in Vietnam.

Table 4 illustrates the multiple significant correlates of the various measures of inpatient dangerousness that were found. All indepen-

Table 3. Significant correlations between hostility and self-destructiveness measures in 80 schizophrenic inpatients

	Self-destructiveness measures		
Hostility measures	Act	Seclusion	Restraint
Observed (Lion scale totals)	—	0.33***	0.54***
Self-report (Buss-Durkee)			
Assault	—	—	—
Indirect	0.35***	—	—
Irritableness	0.23*	—	—
Negativism	0.36***	—	—
Resentment	−0.26***	—	−0.19
Suspicion	−0.19(*)	−0.22*	—
Verbal assault	0.31**	0.21*	—
Buss-Durkee factors			
Indirect hostility factor	—	−0.21*	—
Direct hostility factor	0.41***	0.32***	—

Note. (*)$p < .10$; *$p < .05$ **$p < .01$; ***$p < .005$ (two-tailed).

Table 4. Correlates of dangerousness measures on 70 hospitalized schizophrenics

	Physical assault	Seclusion and restraint	Verbal assaults	Assaults and other acts
Thiothixene serum level	−0.47***	−0.01	−0.33**	−0.38***
Prior violence	0.33**	0.23	0.25*	0.22
Schizophrenia factor on BPRS	0.34**	0.32**	0.27*	0.31**
Combat in Vietnam	0.24*	0.30*	0.28*	0.25*
Childhood discipline	0.24*	0.01	0.07	0.21

Note. $*p < .05$; $**p < .01$; $***p < .005$ (two-tailed).

dent variables tested were significantly correlated with physical assault. Thiothixene serum level, severity of act preceding admission, and BPRS schizophrenia factor score were most highly correlated with physical assaults.

Stepwise multiple regression was then performed on these correlates to determine the relative contribution of each in explaining danger-related behavior. Age, race, and duration of illness were controlled for in the regression. In this statistical procedure, each correlate is entered in the order of the amount of variance of the dependent measure that is accounted for by it. Table 5 gives the cumulative multiple R^2 obtained for each step. The multiple R^2 is a measure of the amount of additional variance explained by each variable as it is added to the regression equation. Only variables that explained significantly ($p < .05$, by F test) more additional variance than what was already accounted for by the variables included in the previous step were included. The beta weights reflect the relative contribution on the dependent variable of each correlate after all have been included in the regression equation.

The best correlates of inpatient assaults were lower serum levels of thiothixene, higher BPRS schizophrenia factor scores, and more severe violence prior to admission. Of particular importance in the findings is the strong correlation of thiothixene serum levels with two of three inpatient danger-related measures as well as with the summary score of all danger-related events. These results suggest that violence by hospitalized schizophrenics is accounted for at least in part by suboptimal blood levels of neuroleptic medication. In fact, 80 percent of the subjects who committed assaults on the ward had serum levels below the group mean. In a separate regression analysis involving data from the same subject group (Yesavage 1984b), a drug abuse history (especially with PCP) was also substantially correlated with physical assaults on the ward.

The importance of these findings lies in their identification of potential predictors of inpatient violence that can be obtained by simple neuroleptic blood level assay and psychiatric interview. Since assaults by hospitalized psychiatric patients are likely to be underreported (Lion et al. 1981) and therefore occur more frequently than is currently acknowledged, early use of such predictors could prevent injury to staff and patients.

It is apparent from Tables 3 and 4, as well as from data presented earlier in this chapter, that correlations were smaller between independent variables and seclusion/restraint episodes than they were with other variables such as physical or verbal assault. This may be accounted for by the fact that the decision to seclude or restrain

Table 5. Regression of dangerousness measures in 70 hospitalized schizophrenics with correlates

Dangerousness measure	Correlates	Cumulative R^2	Standardized β
Physical assaults	Thiothixene serum level	0.22	−0.42
($F = 5.74$, 3/66 df, $p < .01$)	BPRS schizophrenia factor	0.45	0.35
	Violence prior to admit	0.49	0.50
Seclusion and restraint	Vietnam combat	0.09	0.40
($F = 3.63$, 3/66 df, $p < .05$)	Violence prior to admit	0.16	0.28
	BPRS schizophrenia factor	0.24	0.23
Verbal assaults	Thiothixene serum level	0.11	−0.34
($F = 3.78$, 4/65 df, $p < .05$)	Vietnam combat	0.24	0.37
	BPRS schizophrenia factor	0.34	0.37
	Violence prior to admit	0.49	0.35
Inpatient dangerous acts	Thiothixene serum level	0.14	−0.46
($F = 6.43$, 4/65 df, $p < .01$)	BPRS schizophrenia factor	0.36	0.36
	Vietnam combat	0.50	0.38
	Violence prior to admit	0.65	0.21

Note. Negative β for thiothixene serum level indicates that lower serum levels were associated with higher behavioral counts. Other variables included in the analyses that did not significantly correlate with dangerousness were childhood discipline, race, duration of illness, and age.

involves a complex nursing decision and parameters possibly not taken into account in these studies (Yesavage 1984a).

Another approach to improving the accuracy of predictions of violence is to explore the possibility that there may be subgroups of psychotic patients whose "best" predictors differ. One study (Tanke and Yesavage 1985) described two groups of violent inpatients: one consisted of patients whose hostile, suspicious, or excited behavior suggested the potential for violence; the other group was made up of potentially violent patients who did not exhibit these characteristics.

In a study (Tanke and Yesavage 1985) by our group of 289 hospitalized patients with schizophrenia or schizoaffective disorder, BPRS factor scores of "high visibility" violent patients (those who had physical assaults within 24 hours of a preceding verbal assault) were compared with those of "low visibility" violent patients (patients who had no verbal assaults or who had no verbal assaults within 48 hours of a subsequent attack) and with those of nonviolent patients. Only the high visibility patients rated significantly higher on the BPRS hostile-suspiciousness factor. Low visibility patients had significantly higher scores than the nonviolent group on the BPRS withdrawal-retardation factor. These findings suggest that the distinction between high and low visibility violent patients group was a valid one. Further, a discriminant analysis performed on the data for the low visibility patients and the nonviolent patients in the sample who had not engaged in verbal assault suggested that BPRS factor scores can add to the accuracy of predictions of violence among low visibility patients.

ABILITY OF PSYCHIATRISTS AND PSYCHOLOGISTS TO PREDICT INPATIENT VIOLENCE

Findings from two studies (Werner et al. 1983, 1984) from our group suggest that there are differences between cues utilized by clinicians to make predictions of violence and empirical correlates of violence.

In one study (Werner et al. 1983), 30 experienced psychologists and psychiatrists reviewed the BPRS scores and presence or absence of a violent act preceding admission in 40 male inpatients. The DSM-III diagnoses of the patients were as follows: paranoid schizophrenia, 16 patients (40 percent); chronic undifferentiated schizophrenia, 7 (17.5 percent); schizoaffective disorder, 6 (15 percent); manic-depressive disorder, 4 (10 percent); and other diagnoses, 7 (17.5 percent). Overall, judges attained a low accuracy rate in predicting patients' violence (physical assaults documented by nursing staff in patients' charts). Clinicians' predictions of violence utilized the history of assaultiveness prior to admission as well as patients' scores on BPRS hostility and depressive mood scales. Empirical correlates of violence in the patient sample studied included the absence of emotional withdrawal and the presence of hallucinatory behavior (as rated on the BPRS). The apparent discrepancy between this finding and the previously mentioned association (Tanke and Yesavage 1985) between low visibility dangerousness and higher BPRS scores on the withdrawal-retardation item results from the division of the (larger) sample of patients in the latter study into more homogeneous subgroups. The more closely that individual judge's cue-utilization strategy (Szucko and Kleinmuntz 1981) paralleled the empirical relationship of BPRS scale scores with inpatient violence, the more accurate were the judge's predictions.

In a separate analysis (Werner et al. 1984) of cues utilized by 15 experienced psychiatrists in predicting violent behavior in the same patient sample, it emerged that psychiatrists utilized previous assaultiveness history and BPRS hostility, agitation, and suspiciousness scale scores as indices predictive of inpatient violence. Empirical BPRS correlates of assault, however, included hallucinatory behavior and absence of motor retardation and emotional withdrawal. The accuracy of clinical judgments of inpatient dangerousness could possibly be improved by the inclusion of these judgments of easily obtained information such as absence of motor retardation and emotional withdrawal.

CONCLUSION

Taken as a whole, these studies confirm the utility of neuroleptic serum levels, severity of the act preceding admission, BPRS scores, Vietnam combat experience, and childhood discipline as predictors of violence in the patient sample studied. Additional factors significantly correlated with inpatient dangerousness were patients' history of drug abuse, presence of self-destructiveness, and race. It thus appears that within a time-limited (8 days) single setting (the hospital) context, easily obtained data can be successfully applied as valid predictors of inpatient violence. Clinicians' accuracy in the prediction of inpatient violence can be increased by the utilization of cues that parallel empirical correlates of violence. The recognition of subgroups of patients with "non-obvious" but nonetheless actual predilections for violence (such as the low visibility patients described earlier) will also enhance clinicians' predictive ability.

It is likely that other factors contribute to the commission of inpatient violent behavior. Family stress factors, which are extremely difficult to quantify precisely, may play an important role in precipitating violent behavior (Post et al. 1980). Other potential correlates might include certain trait variables measurable by personality inventories, parameters associated with different types of interactions between patients, and biological markers.

As stated at the outset of this chapter, there is a great deal of skepticism regarding clinicians' ability to predict violent behavior. The studies presented in this review, however, are representative of a second generation (Monahan 1984) of prediction research in which sophisticated psychometric and statistical techniques allied with informed clinical judgment enable psychiatrists to make better predictions. The further understanding and characterization of quantifiable factors useful in short-term context-limited prediction of violence will enhance clinicians' predictive ability and hopefully result in increased prevention of injury to staff and patients on inpatient wards.

REFERENCES

American Psychiatric Association: Diagnostic and Statistical Manual of Mental Disorders, 3rd ed (DSM-III). Washington, DC, American Psychiatric Association, 1980

Baron RA: Human Aggression. New York, McGraw-Hill, 1972

Bartko JJ: The intraclass correlation coefficient as a measure of reliability. Psychol Reports 19:3–11, 1966

Bell C: Interface between psychiatry and the law on the issue of murder. J Natl Med Assoc 72:1093–1097, 1980

Blackburn R: Emotionality, extraversion, and aggression in paranoid and nonparanoid schizophrenic offenders. Br J Psychiatry 115:1301–1302, 1968a

Blackburn R: Personality in relation to extreme aggression in psychiatric offenders. Br J Psychiatry 114:821–828, 1968b

Flaherty J, Meagher R: Measuring racial bias in inpatient treatment. Am J Psychiatry 137:679–682, 1980

Jacobsson L, von Knorring L, Mattson B: Controlled trial of penfluridol and thiothixene in the maintenance treatment of chronic schizophrenic syndromes. Acta Psychiatr Scand 54:113–124, 1976a

Jacobsson L, von Knorring L, Mattson B, et al: Penfluridol and thiothixene: dosage, plasma level and changes in psychopathology. Int Pharmacopsychiatry 11:206, 1976b

Kermani EJ: Violent psychiatric patients: a study. Am J Psychother 35:215–225, 1981

Kim JO: Factor analysis, in Statistical Package for the Social Sciences (2nd ed). Edited by Nie H, Hull CH, Jenkins JG, et al. New York, McGraw-Hill, 1975, pp 488–514

Lawson WB, Yesavage JA, Werner PD: Race, violence, and psychopathology. J Clin Psychiatry 45:294–297, 1984

Lion JR: Evaluation and Management of the Violent Patient. Springfield, Ill, Charles C Thomas, 1972

Lion JR, Kenefich DP, Albert J, et al: Clinical Aspects of the Violent Individual. (Task Force Report No. 8.) Washington, DC, American Psychiatric Association, 1974

Lion JR, Synder W, Merrill GL: Underreporting of assaults on staff in a state hospital. Hosp Community Psychiatry 32:497–498, 1981

Megargee EI: The role of inhibition in the assessment and understanding of violence, in The Control of Aggression and Violence: Cognitive and Physiological Factors. Edited by Singer JL. New York, Academic Press, 1971

Monahan J: The Clinical Prediction of Violent Behavior. Rockville, MD, US Department of Health and Human Services, 1981

Monahan J: The prediction of violent behavior: towards a second generation of theory and policy. Am J Psychiatry 141:10–15, 1984

Mullen JM, Dudley HK, Craig EM: Dangerousness and the mentally ill offender. Hosp Community Psychiatry 29:424–425, 1978

Overall JE, Klett CJ: Applied Multivariate Analysis. New York, McGraw-Hill, 1972

Post RD, Willett AB, Franks RD, et al: A preliminary report on the prevalence of domestic violence among psychiatric inpatients. Am J Psychiatry 137:974–975, 1980

Rosenbaum CP, Adams JE, Scott KL, et al: Alcohol and violence: a clinical study, in Biobehavioral Aspects of Aggression. Edited by Hamburg DA, Trudeau MB. New York, Alan R Liss, 1981, pp 169–226

Schneideman ES: Suicide, in Comprehensive Textbook of Psychiatry, Vol 2 (2nd ed). Edited by Freedman AM, Kaplan HI, Sadock BJ. Baltimore, Williams & Wilkins, 1975, pp 1774–1784

Soloff PH, Turner SM: Patterns of seclusion: a prospective study. J Nerv Ment Dis 169:37–44, 1982

Student D, Lion JR: Methodological Issues in Psychopharmacological Research in Violent Individuals. Washington, DC, International Society for Research on Aggression, National Institutes of Medicine, 1978

Szucko JJ, Kleinmuntz B: Statistical versus clinical lie detection. Am Psychol 36:488–496, 1981

Tanke ED, Yesavage JA: Characteristics of assaultive patients who do and do not provide visible cues of potential violence. Am J Psychiatry 142:1409–1413, 1985

Tinklenberg JR, Woodrow KW: Drug use among youthful assaultive and sexual offenders. Agression 52:209–224, 1974

Werner PD, Rose TL, Yesavage JA: Reliability, accuracy, and decision-making strategy in clinical predictions of imminent dangerousness. J Consult Clin Psychol 51:815–825, 1983

Werner PD, Rose TL, Yesavage JA, et al: Psychiatrists' judgments of dangerousness in patients on an acute care unit. Am J Psychiatry 141:263–266, 1984

Yesavage JA: Inpatient violence and the schizophrenic patient: an inverse correlation between danger-related events and neuroleptic levels. Biol Psychiatry 17:1331–1336, 1982

Yesavage JA: Bipolar illness: correlates of dangerous inpatient behavior. Br J Psychiatry 143:554–557, 1983a

Yesavage JA: Dangerous behavior by Vietnam combat veterans with schizophrenia. Am J Psychiatry 140:1180–1183, 1983b

Yesavage JA: Differential effects of Vietnam combat experiences vs criminality on dangerous behavior by Vietnam veterans with schizophrenia. J Nerv Ment Dis 171:382–384, 1983c

Yesavage JA: Inpatient violence and the schizophrenic patient. Acta Psychiatr Scand 67:353–357, 1983d

Yesavage JA: Relationship between measures of direct and indirect hostility and self-destructive behavior by hospitalized schizophrenics. Br J Psychiatry 143:173–176, 1983e

Yesavage JA: Correlates of dangerous behavior by schizophrenics in hospital. J Psychiatr Res 18:225–231, 1984a

Yesavage JA: Plasma levels as predictors of clinical response and violent behavior. J Clin Psychiatry Monograph 2 (No 2):14–20, 1984b

Yesavage JA, Zarcone V: History of drug abuse and dangerous behavior in inpatient schizophrenics. J Clin Psychiatry 44:259–261, 1983

Yesavage JA, Werner PD, Becker J, et al: Inpatient evaluation of aggression in psychiatric patients. J Nerv Ment Dis 169:299–302, 1981

Yesavage JA, Becker J, Werner PD, et al: Serum level monitoring of thiothixene in schizophrenia: acute single dose levels at fixed doses. Am J Psychiatry 139:174–178, 1982a

Yesavage JA, Werner PD, Becker JMT, et al: Short-term civil commitment and the violent patient. Am J Psychiatry 139:1145–1149, 1982b

Yesavage JA, Becker JMT, Werner PD, et al: Family conflict, psychopathology, and dangerous behavior by schizophrenic inpatients. Psychiatry Res 8:271–280, 1983

Chapter 5

Hierarchical Neural Regulation of Aggression: Some Predictable Patterns of Violence

David M. Bear, M.D.

Chapter 5

Hierarchical Neural Regulation of Aggression: Some Predictable Patterns of Violence

D espite often-cited disclaimers by professionals (Monahan 1981), common sense tells us that many violent acts are predictable. No one would be surprised, for example, if someone shouting threats and brandishing a gun subsequently shot an individual. If a patient entered a psychiatrist's office and repeatedly announced intentions to kill the therapist's wife and children, most of us would consider the likelihood of aggression sufficiently high to protect our families.

In addition to our acquired sensitivity to threatening language, we as human beings have inherited the capacity to read aggressive intent from many other cues such as body posture, tone of voice, and facial expression. As Darwin (1896) so beautifully observed, some expressions of anger such as the upturned lip of a snarling person may gain their meaning from the habitual exposure of canine teeth prior to predatory attack or combat among our mammalian progenitors. Within our nervous systems, we have likely encoded both the motor programs to enable the snarl and the sensory circuits that interpret this menacing expression on the faces of others (Bear 1983).

However, some violent acts do seem genuinely surprising and are unpredicted despite our normally accurate emotional surveillance. An example might be a scratching or biting episode of a usually docile young women who later apologized that she had not meant to attack her many victims (Reeves and Plum 1969). As well, it might be unexpected that a deeply religious and intensely moral middle-aged woman would commit multiple aggravated assaults on police officers or telephone death threats against high public officials (Bear et al. 1985b). Another initially perplexing pattern of aggression developed in a young nurse who, having become apathetic about her professional career and emotionally unresponsive to her family, repeatedly burned her young son with cigarette butts (Weiger and Bear 1988).

At first blush, these might be considered examples of unpredicted or even unpredictable aggressive acts. However, I believe that each situation becomes understandable—and in an important sense, predictable—when viewed as a breakdown of specific neuronal systems regulating aggression at multiple levels within the human brain. The appreciation and study of these disparate circuits will not only enhance our ability to predict certain forms of violence but, ultimately, to modify or prevent them.

BIOLOGICAL ORIGINS OF HUMAN AGGRESSION

Aggression in the animal kingdom—the attack of one organism on another—typically occurs in the service of other biologically adaptive behaviors: predation, territorial defense, competition for mates, and protection of offspring (Weiger and Bear 1988). Aggressive behavior originates and is selected for as an instrumentality in consummating biological drives essential for survival of the organism or, more specifically, for propagation of its genetic material (Wilson 1975). Most natural aggressive acts are precisely triggered, limited in scope, and promptly terminated following satiation of the relevant drive.

These general principles lead to useful clinical corollaries. Because there has been no selection pressure for overly frequent or aimless aggression (at least in species other than humans), such acts in humans could and often do reflect structural or chemical dysfunction of inherited neuronal circuits. Because of the close evolutionary, functional, and anatomical relationships relating other biological drives to aggression, organic aggressive syndromes are often distinguished by simultaneous disturbances in such activities as feeding, sexuality, or social affiliation (Weiger and Bear 1988).

NEUROLOGICAL MODULATION OF AGGRESSION

A neuroanatomical fossil record or recapitulation of the evolution of neural structures regulating emotion exists within the primate brain (MacLean 1985). In general, phylogenetically ancient structures are formed first in development, and take up caudal and medial positions. As newer structures develop, they migrate to positions successively more rostral and lateral. Three representative levels of the neuraxis are the brain stem, the limbic lobe, and the neocortex.

Multiple circuits are specialized for control of biological drives such as aggression at each of these levels of the nervous system.

Typically, emotion-controlling circuits are interposed between sensory and motor centers; each level of circuitry relies on particular sensory inputs, specialized output channels, and distinctive principles of integration (Weiger and Bear 1988). As well, newer levels of emotional organization rely on processing by lower levels, resulting in a sequential hierarchical organization for control of biological drives such as aggression (Bear et al. 1985a) (Figure 1). The roles

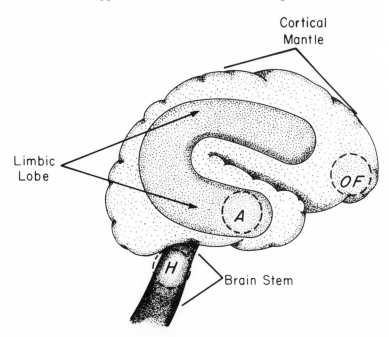

Figure 1.   Hierarchical control of aggression in the human brain. Three gross levels of organization readily distinguished in the human brain are: the brain stem (diencephalon, midbrain, pons, medulla); the limbic lobe (amygdala, hippocampus, cingulate, septal complex); and the cortical mantle (neocortex of frontal, temporal, parietal, and occipital lobes). In both phylogenetic and ontogenetic development, newer structures migrate to positions successively more lateral and rostral, suggesting a functional hierarchy: neocortex ◗ limbic lobe ◗ brain stem. Each level contains aggregations of interneurons regulating aggression and related biological drives. Relative functions of these nuclear structures are understood by considering their afferents, efferents, and principles of functional regulation. H = hypothalamus, A = amygdaloid complex, OF = orbital prefrontal cortex.

of the hypothalamus, amygdaloid complex, and orbital prefrontal cortex in aggression will be compared and contrasted, and case examples of aggression resulting from disturbances in each of these brain systems will be presented.

HYPOTHALAMIC CONTROL OF BIOLOGICAL DRIVES AND AGGRESSION

Sensory input to the primate hypothalamus is focused on the internal milieu (the oral cavity, visceral organs such as heart and gut, and the chemical and osmotic composition of the bloodstream). The direct outputs of the hypothalamus are to the autonomic nervous system, the pituitary gland controlling neuroendocrine responses, and to midbrain and spinal motor centers, which elicit stereotypic movements. In regulating a biological drive such as feeding, the hypothalamus relies on a hard-wired or innate antagonism of excitatory and inhibitory nuclei (push-pull control). Neurophysiological comparisons lead to homeostatic or stereotyped drive responses, which are not modified by prior experience. For example, stimulation of the lateral hypothalamic area initiates feeding in the rat; stimulation of the ventromedial area rapidly terminates eating; high glucose levels are stimulatory to the ventromedial and result in inhibition of the lateral area; and lesions of the lateral hypothalamus can lead to starvation, whereas chemical destruction or electrical lesion of the ventromedial area results in obesity (Weiger and Bear 1988).

In nonhuman species, the principle of "on or off" elicitation of stereotypic response appears to apply to aggression. Following cortical ablation, stimulation of the posterior lateral hypothalamus of the cat elicits "sham rage," a combination of hissing, piloerection, mydriasis, and extension of the claws that represents preparation for attack. By contrast, stimulation of the medial ventral area elicits defensive posturing. In the intact brain, stimulation of the posterior lateral hypothalamus will shorten the latency for attack by a cat on a rat, whereas stimulation of medial ventral areas will prolong this latency (Weiger and Bear 1988).

Attack behavior can be facilitated by instillation of specific neurotransmitters such as acetylcholine, which will promote biting attack of a rat on a mouse or a frog, or of a cat on a mouse or a rat; cholinergic blockers will eliminate biting attacks even in naturally aggressive cats or rats (Smith et al. 1970; Weiger and Bear 1988). These well-established observations regarding hypothalamic control of aggression in animals provide a basis for understanding hypothalamic aggressive syndromes in man.

Examples

A 20-year-old woman developed bulimia and became strikingly obese; she was amenorrheic and acquired diabetes insipidus. When reevaluated approximately 2 years later, her behavior included outbursts of aggression. During these episodes she would indiscriminately hit, scratch, or bite multiple examiners who approached her; she often expressed regret for these unprovoked attacks. While the violent behavior was not targeted against specific individuals, it appeared to be more frequent during intervals when she had not eaten. Other endocrine and autonomic problems included hypothyroidism, adrenal cortical hypofunction, hypogonadism, and episodic pyrexia. At autopsy, a 0.5 × 1.5 cm hamartoma was seen to have destroyed the ventromedial hypothalamus bilaterally (Reeves and Plum 1969).

A middle-aged medical scientist dusted his pets with a tick powder containing carbaryl, a potent inhibitor of acetylcholinesterase. Within several days, he and a housemate noted the onset of stalking behavior in his cat, which began to kill large numbers of birds and mice; the cat exhibited classic predatory behavior by killing its victims with a bite through the high cervical spinal cord. At the same time, the scientist developed a "continual rage" that led to uncharacteristic violent arguments on any subject accompanied by flushing and threatening behavior. His aggressiveness was sufficiently worrisome that a long-time intimate companion fled the home out of fear of physical attack. Within a week of terminating the use of the carbaryl, the aggressive symptoms ceased in both cat and man (Bear et al. 1986). Other reports have linked anticholinesterase intoxication with a lowered threshold for aggression and precipitation of homicide (Weiger and Bear 1988).

THE AMYGDALA AND CONTROL OF AGGRESSION

In contrast to the hypothalamus, the primate amygdala receives input from multiple sensory systems involved in exploring the external world. In particular, visual cortex within the temporal lobe, which is specialized for object recognition in central vision, projects extensively to the basolateral sector of the amygdala (Bear 1983). Primary outputs of the amygdala include the extrapyramidal motor system and the hypothalamus (Bear 1983).

Many observations suggest a fundamental role of the amygdala in relating sensory experiences such as the visual discrimination of specific objects to biological drives such as aggression. The two limbic structures within the temporal lobe—the amygdala and the hippocampus—play a fundamental role in new learning and memory; the amygdala may be particularly relevant for recall of the affective significance of previously encountered stimuli (Bear 1983).

Following bilateral removal of the anterior temporal lobe in monkeys, dramatic behavior changes develop including the eating of junk objects, loss of selectivity in choosing sexual partners, and suppression of fear responses: this has been codified as the Kluver-Bucy syndrome (Kluver and Bucy 1939). With regard to aggression, removal of the amygdala in most monkeys results in taming and placidity. However, amygdalectomy in submissive monkeys can lead to retention or increase in aggression, suggesting that the fundamental effect of amygdalectomy is not simply a change in the threshold of aggression but may involve modification of the previous pathways associating stimuli with aggressive responses. For example, after hemisphere disconnection, unilateral amygdalectomy results in loss of aggressive responses to visual stimuli processed within the operated hemisphere; the animal remains normally aggressive to objects presented in the contralateral visual field (Downer 1961).

In humans, bilateral temporal lobe damage has led to aspects of the Kluver-Bucy syndrome, including the loss of aggressive responses (Marlowe et al. 1975). A far more common clinical syndrome is the class of conditions variously termed *temporal lobe epilepsy* or *complex partial seizure disorder*, in which abnormal neuronal excitability frequently develops within the limbic structures. Patients are rarely aggressive during individual complex partial seizures. However, more recent study has focused on the interictal behavior and emotion of patients with a temporal lobe epileptic focus. An "interictal behavior syndrome" of temporal lobe epilepsy has been described, which includes deepening of many emotions, a sensitivity to moral issues (often with religious and philosophical preoccupation), and a tendency to write about these subjects at length. Such patients may be specially sensitive to slights or violations of principle and may experience intense anger. Strong moral and philosophical beliefs often preclude violent acts, but if patients do act aggressively, their behavior is performed in clear consciousness and is often followed by sincere regret (Devinsky and Bear 1984).

Examples

A middle-aged woman suffered complex partial seizures from childhood. These began with her perception of a foul odor, followed by focal movement of the left face and arm, which occasionally progressed to a secondarily generalized tonic-clonic convulsion. Multiple electroencephalograms (EEGs) revealed an epileptic focus over the right anterior temporal lobe; spike bursts were later recorded from indwelling electrodes within the right amygdala. A stereotactic radio frequency lesion within the right amygdala produced no apparent change in seizure pattern or interictal behavior.

As an adult, the patient wrote extensively, producing more than 30 spiral notebooks filled with somber commentary on her epilepsy, suicidal ideation, and religious interpretations of the Old and New Testaments. These essays were punctuated by angry diatribes against former physicians, politicians, and those who she felt had mistreated her. Her hypergraphia was especially remarkable because deforming rheumatoid arthritis forced her to write with wrist and finger supports; in one diary she noted: "My hands are so sore but I have to just write." Religious preoccupation was also reflected in recorded audio cassettes of personalized sermons on the Bible, which she carried about in large sachels.

Despite her understandable depressive reaction and sincere moral and religious reflections, this patient was recurrently threatening or overtly aggressive. On one occasion, she beat a policeman into unconsciousness for "shameful" sexual innuendos; on another she attempted to castrate an unsatisfying sexual partner. She has been prosecuted for multiple aggravated assaults. Years later, after arthritis confined her to a wheelchair, she became incensed during a State of the Union Address by the President's "total disregard for the poor"; she thereupon telephoned an assassination threat to federal officials (Bear et al. 1985b).

A 40-year-old man, who had experienced recurrent high fevers in childhood, developed attacks of flushing, tachycardia, diaphoresis, and fear beginning in his 20s. Extensive medical examination revealed a dilated temporal horn of the left lateral ventricle and spike discharges over both temporal lobes.

Approximately 18 months after the onset of his autonomic (simple partial) seizures, the patient's military records documented the onset of multiple forms of aggression. Intensely self-critical, he furiously punched his right hand against a door frame, breaking several knuckles. He was subsequently imprisoned for fights with fellow servicemen triggered by a sense that they were "laughing at him or not taking him seriously." Believing he had not received a fair hearing in military court, he systematically destroyed the plumbing fixtures within his stockade cell. When called again before the magistrate he promised, on his release, to murder the judge. After a medical review led to his release from prison, he successfully controlled his temper for many years, developing deep religious and philosophical convictions that proscribed the use of violence. Nonetheless, when questioned about his temper, the patient responded: "I have more of a problem with anger than anybody I've ever met in my life." He then emphasized a constant conflict between vindictive feelings, elicited by a sense of being humiliated or treated unjustly, and a strict moral code that precluded physical attack on any human being. His moral and religious convictions were so compelling that he volunteered to change linen and clean bedpans on a hospital ward, and he lectured to other patients extensively about the clash between God and the Devil in the modern world (Devinsky and Bear 1984).

THE PREFRONTAL CORTEX AND CONTROL OF AGGRESSION

The prefrontal cortex receives afferents from multiple neocortical association areas. There is extensive input from the inferior parietal lobule, an area of the primate brain involved in surveying extrapersonal space for relevant stimuli (Jacobson et al. 1978; Kievit and Kuypers 1975). Projections from the hypothalamus via the dorsal medial nucleus of the thalamus and from temporal limbic structures via the uncinate fasciculus potentially inform the frontal lobe of both the internal milieu and the presence of external stimuli of affective significance (Kievit and Kuypers 1975; Tobias 1975). Major outputs include the pyramidal motor system mediating skilled movements and language, the extrapyramidal motor system, limbic structures such as the amygdala, and the hypothalamus (Leichnetz and Astruc 1975; Randya et al. 1971).

Functionally, the prefrontal cortex appears to interpret events in the external world, the state of the internal milieu, and the appearance of emotion-associated stimuli in the light of previous experience relating to biological drives. A fundamental role of the frontal lobe is to construct a behavioral plan consistent with prior experience and acquired social rules to optimize satisfaction of the biological drives (Bear et al. 1985a).

In humans, damage to the dorsal convexity of the frontal lobe results in an absence of long-term behavioral planning—a state characterized as apathy or abulia. Damage to the orbital undersurface more frequently results in superficial, reflexive emotional responses to stimuli without consideration of long-term, socially prescribed consequences (Bear et al. 1985a; Blumer and Benson 1975).

The frontal lobe personality syndrome includes characteristic forms of aggression. Such patients may be transiently irritable, often striking out after trivial provocation. The anger is quickly forgotten and there is little consideration for the ramifications of such behavior (Bear et al. 1985a; Blumer and Benson 1975).

Examples

Following episodes of blurred vision, right-sided weakness, and truncal ataxia, a middle-aged nurse abruptly lost interest in work, home care, and maternal responsibilities for two young children. A computed tomography (CT) scan revealed an extensive lesion within the right prefrontal cortex, which was interpreted as a demylinating placque associated with multiple sclerosis.

During a typical day, the patient was awakened by her morning alarm but did not arise or dress for work. She spent hours lying in bed and was inattentive to the needs of her family, although she denied feeling depressed. She was often incontinent of urine but showed no embarrassment when the bedclothes had to be changed.

She was generally apathetic, expressing little spontaneous affection for her mother or children. By contrast, when food was presented, she became attentive and ate wolfishly.

She showed little spontaneous anger or temper. However, questions or exhortations from family members led to sharp verbal retorts often accompanied by attempts to push away her interlocutor. She was particularly irritated by the cries of her young son and abruptly burned his arms with lighted cigarette butts on several occasions. When he fled from the room, she denied any lingering anger but showed no concern for the serious injuries she had caused (Weiger and Bear 1988).

SUMMARY

This chapter has illustrated contrasting patterns of aggression that may result from neurological processes affecting specific pathways within the neuraxis. The patterns become more understandable and therefore potentially predictable from an analysis of the inputs received by differing neural structures, the nature of their major efferents, and a consideration of the logic or principles of decision making applied by the hypothalamus, amygdala, or prefrontal cortex. These relationships are contrasted in Table 1.

The concept of multiple hierarchical neural controls over aggression may extend our knowledge and ability to predict human violence. In introducing this viewpoint, however, many simplifications are necessarily involved. Thus examples of aggression that clearly developed de novo after unambiguous brain lesions were chosen. Three particular anatomical structures and one neurotransmitter system have been chosen as illustrative rather than exhaustive paradigms. Obviously, one cannot reduce the human brain—much less a living human being with a complex interpersonal history—to the operation of selected neuronal circuits.

To extend this mode of analysis, one must consider not only the important interactions of environment with organic abnormality, but the possibility of coexisting lesions in multiple levels of neurocircuitry. An unfortunately common setting for combined neural lesions is head trauma, which may result in contusion to the orbital frontal cortex while creating a posttraumatic temporo-limbic epileptic focus. The resulting changes in behavior often reflect complementary fea-

Table 1. Contrasting roles of hypothalamus, amygdala, and prefrontal cortex in regulation of aggression

Anatomical level	Illustrative structure	Predominant incoming information	Major outflow	Principles of normal functioning	Associated aggressive syndromes in humans
Brain stem	Hypothalamus	Interoceptive (chemical, osmotic, visceral)	Neuroendocrine; autonomic; stereotypic motor (midbrain and pontine centers)	Quantitative regulation of biological drives (feeding aggression); coordinating unlearned stereotypic responses; hard-wired circuits involving characteristic neurotransmitters common to humans and animals	Destructive lesions of ventromedial hypothalamus: indiscriminant rage attacks with stereotypic scratching and biting; autonomic and neuroendocrine abnormalities; verbal regret for behavior. Hypothalamic pattern precipitable by cholinergic agonists (?); syndromes include associated neuroendocrine changes, obesity, pyrexia, diabetes insipidus; alteration of REM-NREM sleep stages
Limbic lobe	Amygdala	Exteroceptive (visual, auditory, somatosensory)	Hypothalamus, extrapyramidal motor system	Association of biological drives with specific stimuli; learning and retrieval of stimulus-response bonds	Destructive lesions: placidity ± infrequent poorly targeted aggression; epileptic activation during interictal period (interictal behavior syndrome of temporolimbic epilepsy); concern with injustice; moralistic sensitivity; deeply felt targeted anger; angry feelings often clash with strong moral/religious ideation
Cortical mantle	Orbital prefrontal cortex	Multiple exteroceptive sources (central and peripheral, interoceptive sources)	Pyramidal motor system enabling skilled motor movements, language	Construction of multiple-step temporally extended behavioral program to maximize satisfaction of biological drives; application of elaborate social rules for expression of emotions such as anger	Orbital lesions: transient aggressive outbursts in setting of superficial emotionality; little consideration for consequences of aggressive actions

tures of the individual behavioral syndromes. Thus anger may be experienced intensely and targeted on particular individuals (as an aspect of the interictal behavior syndrome of temporo-limbic epilepsy), while loss of concern for the consequences of actions resulting from orbital frontal damage removes an important restraining mechanism over aggressive behavior (Weiger and Bear 1988). Two final examples serve to illustrate the behavioral consequences of multiple foci of neural damage.

Examples

Following a limb fracture, a young man sustained a severe closed-head injury when the ambulance in which he was riding collided with an automobile. Examination documented epileptic spiking in the left amygdala and structural damage to both frontal lobes. Over a period of months he became, according to his devout parents, a "religious fanatic" who was rejected by the Jehovah's Witness movement as overzealous. He kept a voluminous diary of religious writings in which he labeled his former girlfriends as the agents of Satan. He did not appreciate his social inappropriateness or the effects of his menacing behavior. He was finally hospitalized after attempting to murder his parents.

A well-known serial murderer, recently studied by CT and magnetic resonance imaging (MRI), has coexisting lesions in temporal and frontal cortex (Weiger and Bear 1988).

It is not the conclusion of this chapter that all aggression has an organic or structural basis. Rather, it is to be hoped that an anatomico-physiological analysis may clarify the nature of interactions between environment, learning, and neural structure at various levels of the nervous system. For example, the hypothalamus may differ little in anatomy or neurochemistry across many mammalian species; it does not appear to be modifiable by experience. On the other hand, afferents to the primate amygdala diverge extensively between the rat and higher primates; the temporo-limbic structures are critically involved in learning, on the basis of experience, specific aggressive associations. The prefrontal association cortex is perhaps the most uniquely human brain region, having expanded more than sevenfold between humans and chimpanzees; this heterogeneous structure must incorporate over many years of painful development the complex and sometimes conflicting social generalizations regarding appropriate expression of emotions such as anger. The availability of appropriate environmental models for impulse control are as essential to the successful operation of the adult frontal lobe as are its complement of neurotransmitters.

REFERENCES

Bear D: Hemispheric specialization and the neurology of emotion. Arch Neurol 40:195–208, 1983

Bear D, Freeman R, Greenberg M: Alterations in personality associated with neurologic illnesses. Psychiatry 1:1–13, 1985a

Bear DM, Freeman R, Greenberg M, et al: Psychiatric aspects of temporal lobe epilepsy. American Psychiatric Association Annual Review 4:190–210, 1985b

Bear D, Rosenbaum J, Norman R: Aggression in cat and man precipitated by cholinesterase inhibitor. Psychosomatics 26:535–536, 1986

Blumer D, Benson DF: Personality changes with frontal and temporal lobe lesions. Psychiatric Aspects of Neurologic Disease 1:151–170, 1975

Darwin C (1896): The Expression of Emotions in Man and Animals. New York, Appleton Press, 1965

Devinsky O, Bear DM: Varieties of aggressive behavior in temporal lobe epilepsy. Am J Psychiatry 141:651–656, 1984

Downer JL: Changes in visual gnostic functions and emotional behaviour following unilateral temporal pole damage in the "split-brain" monkey. Nature 191:50–51, 1961

Jacobson S, Butters N, Tovsky NJ: Afferent and efferent subcortical projections of behaviorally defined sectors of prefrontal granular cortex. Brain Res 159:279–296, 1978

Kievit J, Kuypers H: Basal forebrain and hypothalamic connections to frontal and parietal cortex in the rhesus monkey. Science 187:660–662, 1975

Kluver H, Bucy PC: Preliminary analysis of functions of the temporal lobes in monkeys. Archives of Neurology and Psychiatry 42:979–1000, 1939

Leichnetz GR, Astruc J: Efferent connections of the orbitofrontal cortex in the marmoset (saguinus oedipus). Brain Res 84:169–180, 1975

MacLean P: Brain evolution relating to family, play, and the separation call. Arch Gen Psychiatry 42:405–417, 1985

Marlowe WB, Mancall EL, Thomas JJ: Complete Kulver-Bucy syndrome in man. Cortex 11:53–59, 1975

Monahan J: Predicting Violent Behavior. Beverly Hills, Calif., Sage Publications, 1981

Pandya PN, Dye P, Butters N: Efferent cortico-cortical projections of the prefrontal cortex in the rhesus monkey. Brain Res 31:35–46, 1971

Reeves AG, Plum F: Hyperphagia, rage and dementia accompanying a ventromedial hypothalamic neoplasm. Arch Neurol 20:616–624, 1969

Smith DE, King MD, Hoebel BG: Lateral hypothalamic control of killing: evidence for a cholinoceptive mechanism. Science 167:900–901, 1970

Tobias JJ: Afferents to prefrontal cortex from the thalamic mediodorsal nucleus in the rhesus monkey. Brain Res 83:191–212, 1975

Weiger B, Bear D: An approach to the neurology of aggression. J Psychiatr Res 22:85–98, 1988

Wilson EO: Sociobiology: The New Synthesis. Cambridge, Mass., Harvard University Press, 1975

Chapter 6

Environmental Concomitants of Psychiatric Inpatient Violence

Martha Crowner, M.D.

Chapter 6

Environmental Concomitants of Psychiatric Inpatient Violence

With a quick review of the chapters in this volume it becomes clear that the prediction of violence has made substantial progress but is still far from ideal. As Monahan (1984) has suggested, prediction may improve when studies are expanded to include situational variables. To date, most prediction studies have focused on state and trait variables with, at most, passing mention of the external context. As with all behavior, violent behavior is best understood as the result of an interaction between a person's enduring traits and immediate state of mind, and the interpersonal and environmental setting.

The purpose of this chapter is to consider situational concomitants of violence committed by psychiatric patients in the hospital. These associations cannot yet be accurately called predictors because prediction studies have not been done; even the study of situational associations has barely begun. Many papers from many theoretical perspectives mention situational factors in conjunction with patient factors or in the process of making treatment recommendations. This chapter will present a review of anecdotes and data gathered from the general psychiatric literature on inpatient violence. Occasionally, studies using different populations in different settings will be mentioned briefly, but only to flesh out a conceptual background. The environment will be defined broadly but some aspects will be arbitrarily excluded. Factors in the interval environment such as blood glucose level and drug and alcohol intoxications will be excluded. Cultural background, socioeconomic status, and personal history will not be considered environmental factors but trait factors. The relationship between violence and time elapsed since admission will also be excluded. This relationship may be revealing, however. According to Dietz and Rada's (1983) work, there is evidence that assaults are more likely soon after admission or among patients with particularly prolonged hospitalizations.

This chapter will discuss psychodynamic, ethological, and behavioral perspectives on possible situational correlates of inpatient violence. It will also consider the frustration-aggression hypothesis and possible interpersonal provocations or frustrations. It will present data on the associations between assaults and certain times of day, certain locations, patient density, and structured activity. Finally, there will be a short discussion of cues or recognizable preludes to assaults.

Psychodynamic Perspectives

Authors with a psychodynamic orientation are concerned with conscious or unconscious feelings on the part of staff or patients that may promote or provoke inpatient violence. Their insights are often based on years of clinical experience with violent patients (Lion and Pasternak 1973; Lion et al. 1976) or on careful review of collections of incident reports. The literature usually takes the form of case reports with discussions. Most papers address the problem of violence in a broad psychiatric population; a few consider more limited populations. Few papers describe experimental studies.

Many authors stress the importance of effective limit setting, that is, communicating and enforcing rules for proper behavior. Firm and consistent limit setting may calm the potentially assaultive patient and the patient's peers. According to Lion and Pasternak (1973), "Since patients with aggressive urges fear losing control of such urges, they become even more agitated when they sense that everyone is afraid of them" (p. 209). Patients who may strike preemptively due to fear of attack from others may also be reassured (Felthous 1984). Consistency and confidence are key. When staff feel internal conflicts about taking on an authoritarian role (Adler et al. 1983) or when they are divided among themselves (Adler et al. 1983) or demoralized (Lion and Madden 1976), there is a greater risk of violence. However, rules should be realistic as well as clear. Overly restrictive, arbitrary, or contradictory rules can be intolerable (Conn and Lion 1983).

Early limit setting may prevent escalation. Erickson and Realmuto (1983) reviewed all seclusion reports from a 4-year period on an adolescent inpatient unit where approximately half the population carried the sole diagnosis of personality disorder. They concluded that the unusually high number of seclusions in 1 year could be partly explained by lack of intervention prior to seclusion. Since staff were unresponsive to disruptive behavior, patients' behavior escalated until staff responded.

Enforcing accountability is a type of limit setting. Some patients may assume that a psychiatric diagnosis is exculpatory (Felthous 1984) or carries an expectation of violent behavior (Dietz and Rada 1983). When they are forced to take responsibility for violent behavior, such behavior may diminish. After relating a case report of a woman with "a tumultuous history of chronic illness" who was billed for repair of ward windows and thereafter showed a marked decrease in destructiveness, Gutheil and Rivinus (1977) concluded that lack of accountability promotes violence. Schwartz and Greenfield (1978) drew similar conclusions after relating the case of a patient with hysterical personality disorder who was tried and convicted for an assault on a nurse.

Another group (Levy and Hartocolis 1976) hypothesized that staff's expectations that patients will become violent, as reflected in the assignment of large male aides, provokes violence. They compared rates of violence on two psychiatric units within the same private facility: one staffed entirely by female nurses and aides (the experimental condition) and a second staffed with both female and male nursing staff (the control ward). Both were long-term voluntary treatment wards where the primary diagnosis was borderline personality disorder. After a year, investigators counted 13 episodes of physical assault on others on the control ward but none on the experimental ward. It is unclear if patients were randomly assigned to the two wards.

Depp (1983) believed that staff expectations that a patient will not improve can be provocative. After conducting structured interviews with the staff members from St. Elizabeth's Hospital most closely involved with 60 assaults that resulted in injuries requiring medical attention, he found staff pessimism concerning therapeutic progress or discharge to be associated with 48 percent of patient assaulters. In 35 percent of cases, staff were hopeful about patient improvement and in 16 percent they were uncertain. Staff pessimism tended to be associated with failure to reassess management after an assault. Depp suggested that staff hopelessness and passivity can have hostile components and so represent a form of provocation.

Staff feelings may provoke patient violence in other ways. Staff may subtly encourage acting out to fulfill their own violent fantasies. They may project rageful feelings onto a patient, reject the patient, and then provoke or encourage violence to precipitate transfer to another facility (Felthous 1984). Staff avoidance of the feelings evoked by assaultive patients can lead to a tendency to treat them solely as dispositional problems, thus forestalling therapeutic efforts (Lion and Madden 1976). Denial can lead staff to ignore warnings or to avoid taking action once violence has occurred (Adler et al. 1983; Felthous 1984).

Changes in staffing may provoke violence as patients respond to staff turmoil or to feelings of abandonment. Erickson and Realmuto (1983) related the timing of riots on an adolescent unit to absences of both the unit director and a faculty member on one occasion, and to the interim between the director's resignation and his replacement on another. Depp (1983) agreed that changes in significant staff members may contribute to violence but could not find such an association in his study. He attributed this to the low frequency of staff departures.

Patients' feelings toward each other may lead to violence through scapegoating. Scapegoated peers may become targets through displacement of feelings toward staff (Felthous 1984) or as a defense against threats to psychological stability brought on by proximity to very disorganized psychotic patients (Ionno 1983).

Patients may be caught up in a contagion of violence, perhaps due to blurring of ego boundaries (Marohn 1982). Tardiff (1983) has noted that "minor incidents often escalate on the wards either in the same patient or in contagion to other patients" and that "assault breeds assaults" (p. 15). In his study of assaults on a ward for severely disturbed female patients in a private facility, Ionno (1983) found clustering of events. When three or more assaults occurred on the same day, they usually all occurred within a single 3- to 6-hour time period and were not due to the repetitive assaults of individual patients. Depp's (1983) finding that 29 of 60 wards reported only zero to two incidents within 30 days was interpreted as not supporting the contagion hypothesis. Depp allowed that "contagion is certainly subject to differing operational definitions and requires a formal comparison between adjacent time periods to argue persuasively for its presence or absence" (p. 30).

Quinsey and Varney (1977) followed Depp's (1983) suggestion and employed sophisticated analytic procedures, including the interresponse time per opportunity statistic. They also found no support for the contagion hypothesis. As part of a study of assaults over a 1-year period at a maximum security forensic hospital, they focused on one ward, the ward where most assaults occurred. They found little change in the probability of an assault as a function of time since the last assault.

Ethological Perspectives

Konrad Lorenz, a prominent ethological theoretician, held that instinctive aggression is present in all animals and serves purposes of the species as a whole: population disposal, optimal use of natural resources, and natural selection (Lorenz 1966). Many would argue that human aggression is not instinctive (Montagu 1976) and that concepts borrowed from ethology cannot be applied to humans. Nevertheless, some have tried to apply the ethological concepts of territoriality and the dominance hierarchy to the understanding of violence among psychiatric inpatients.

Esser (1970) intensively studied the interpersonal behavior of a small group of male chronic psychiatric patients in a research ward dayroom. He constructed an interactional hierarchy (akin to a dominance hierarchy) among patients and mapped out patients' territories. He concluded that patients with territories tended to dominate others within their territories and that higher-ranked patients tended to dominate lower-ranked patients. Esser did not study violence per se but dominance behaviors, defined as a broad range of behaviors including ordering others about, pushing others aside at the water fountain, and denying requests for cigarettes. He did not separately analyze assaults.

In Depp's (1983) study, staff reported the existence of a ward pecking order, in terms of rights, privileges, and status, in their analysis of the circumstances of 30 assaults out of 60. In the other 30 cases, they did not believe a pecking order was present. In 16 of the 30 cases where a hierarchy was reported, the assaulters had a higher status than the victim. In 9 cases the victim had a higher status. In 5 cases the combatants had equal status. Overall, 50 percent of the assaulters came from the upper third of the ward hierarchy but only 7 percent of the victims came from the upper third.

The word *crowding* may imply patients' feelings of intrusion into their territories. In Harris and Varney's (1986) study of 1,172 assaults in a forensic facility, assaulters offered crowding as the only reason for the incident in 2.6 percent of cases. Staff gave this reason in only 1 percent of cases. However, crowding was not defined. (Crowding is also discussed later.)

Modeling and Reinforcement

Modeling is a process of shaping behavior by imitation. To illustrate: in an experiment with normal children, Bandura et al. (1963) exposed three groups to three different tapes of other children behaving aggressively. In one tape the behavior was rewarded, in another it was punished, and in a third it was treated neutrally. Afterward, the group that had seen aggression rewarded had significantly more aggressive play. Those who witnessed aggression punished did not show significantly more or less aggressive play. Ward behavior may be influenced by modeling when violent patients are rewarded with social dominance, cigarettes, or food (Wong et al. 1985).

This issue may bear on the controversy surrounding the effects of violent television and movies. Dietz and Rada (1983) report that an associate at their forensic facility, Dr. Bruce Harry, found that physical assaults increased significantly after patients viewed adventure films (although none were graphically violent) but did not after watching comedies or romances.

Violent behavior may also be directly, instead of vicariously, reinforced. Wong et al. (1985) asserted that "the environmental events that occur after aggressive acts are perhaps the strongest determinants of the probability of future aggression" (p. 25). Positive reinforcers are events that happen after a certain behavior that effectively increase its probability of recurrence (e.g., getting tasty food after bar pressing). Negative reinforcers also increase the probability of a behavior's occurrence; however, they are noxious events that can be avoided after the target behavior occurs (e.g., when electric shock is avoided by bar pressing).

In children, Patterson et al. (1967) found that if a child had successfully retaliated after a chance attack by another child, the first child would more likely be the aggressor in the future. Successful retaliation could be seen as a positive reinforcer, increasing the probability of future aggression. Since brawnier children are more likely to be successful combatants, Patterson et al.'s work suggests how muscularity and aggression might be related in children. Such a relationship may also exist in a different population, adult psychiatric patients, as evidenced by Depp's (1983) study. He found that among the 230 incidents at St. Elizabeth's Hospital in which only one patient was physically aggressive and in which his victim required medical attention, assaulters tended to be heavier than victims.

On a psychiatric ward, reinforcers may be different for different patients and may be inadvertently provided by staff. Injections may represent positive reinforcers because they result in physical stimulation and increased attention from staff (Wong et al. 1985). Seclusion may result in more aggressive behavior because it represents avoidance of a negative reinforcer, noisy and irritating peers (Wong et al. 1985). Negative reinforcement can also occur when staff stop pressing a patient to comply with ward routine (e.g., taking a shower) when he becomes threatening or assaultive (Franzen and Lovell 1987).

The Frustration-Aggression Hypothesis

The frustration-aggression hypothesis is a drive model that holds that aggression is the result of obstruction of goal-directed activity, that is, frustration (Shaffer et al. 1980). Others (Berkowitz 1978) contend that it is simply pain and unpleasantness (often associated with frustration) that provoke aggression. Studies in normal children (Barker et al. 1941) support the idea that deprivation, in one case operationalized as being denied access to attractive toys, makes aggressive play more likely.

In other experimental studies, Azrin et al. (1965, 1966) found that pain and the withdrawal of food can elicit aggression. A number of noxious stimuli have been implicated in the behavioral literature, including crowding, noise, boredom, teasing, insults, and rough-housing (Wong et al. 1985). Franzen and Lovell (1987) stated that punishment itself often elicits aggressive behavior. Antecedents can be specific to patient vulnerabilities, such as the stress of verbal communication for an aphasic patient.

Aggression can be seen as an adjunct behavior, one that occurs regardless of the contingencies (Franzen and Lovell 1987). Adjunct behaviors are likely to occur in a situation "where escape is impossible and when the set of contingencies governing reinforcement is changed" (Franzen and Lovell 1987, p. 390).

Possible Interpersonal Provocations

Interpersonal provocations may be grouped as "noxious stimuli" and considered with the frustration-aggression hypothesis. They are often referred to as "reasons" for assault but evidence for causality is not systematic and usually does not extend beyond a relationship retrospectively inferred by involved staff or patients. Interpersonal precipitants can be between patients or between staff and patients.

Patient-initiated provocations may be common. After conducting interviews with patients and staff, Straker et al. (1977) concluded that patients tended to react to threats from other patients with physical retaliation. In his discussion of assaults at Bellevue Psychiatric Hospital, Kalogerakis (1971) mentioned the unwitting or deliberate provocation of a wide variety of disturbed peers as a factor that can upset the balance between aggressive impulses and controls. He does not describe the provocations in more detail. Fottrell (1980) concluded that the behavior of acutely disturbed patients can be conducive to violence. Kalogerakis implicated both disorganized and deliberate provocation whereas Fottrell may only be referring to the unintentional. Branon (1948), in describing two all-male forensic wards with a varied diagnostic mix, blamed intentional provocations instigated by sociopaths for causing most disruptions. The sociopath was well known for planning escapes, openly defying rules, and "taking great delight in teasing and taunting a psychiatric patient until he blows up" (p. 134).

Staff actions are also noted as precipitants, although less frequently than patient actions. In their review of incident reports, Pearson et al. (1986) found that when staff on acute-care wards noted precipitants of assaults, those most common were that the assailant had been forceably medicated or detained on the ward. (On chronic wards the most common precipitants noted were conflicts over food and personal space.) Fottrell (1980) also believed that being prevented from leaving the ward could lead to patient violence. Stockman and Heiber (1980) found more incidents, of many kinds, in a forensic facility on the day that decisions were made and relayed to patients regarding transfer and competency to stand trial.

In studies that list patient or staff opinions regarding concomitants or reasons for assault, both staff- and patient-initiated factors figure prominently. Harris and Varney (1986) interviewed patient assaulters and staff to solicit their views. Each respondent was allowed only one response for each incident. Agreement between the two parties on reasons for a particular assault was above chance, but low, especially when staff were involved in the assaults. The second most common response given by assaulters (after no response) was that the patient had been "teased or bugged" (20.5 percent of 1,172 replies). Staff gave this as a reason in only 6.4 percent of cases. The only other patient-initiated reason listed was sexual approach, given by 0.5 percent of assaulters and 0.3 percent of staff. Having been provoked by staff was a reason given by 12.0 percent of assaulters, but only 0.2 percent of staff. Having been ordered to do something was less frequently offered as a reason by patients (4.8 percent), but represented the second most common staff response (16.8 percent, after 58.6 percent for no reason/unknown). Anger with ward rules was the reason given by 2.2 percent of assaulters and 5.5 percent of staff members. Quinsey and Varney (1977) found very similar results in another study at the same institution.

Depp (1983) used a structured questionnaire with 143 items to interview the staff members most closely involved with each of 60 violent incidents. He selected incidents occurring on the general adult wards of St. Elizabeth's Hospital between 7:30 and 11:30 A.M. on weekdays. All incidents required medical attention. None were self-directed. Based on his interviews, he listed 25 characteristics that were described as "situations that precede, accompany, or follow violence" (p. 26), where each assault could have more than one descriptor. In 37 percent of the 60 incidents, an "unusually intrusive and meddlesome" victim was described. In 55 percent this factor was combined with "an unusual problem in having others near or touching him or her" in the assailant. Preceding 38 percent of assaults "either or both patients had a privilege request refused or were being actively considered for a privilege change."

Conn and Lion (1983) classified 61 assaults occurring on the psychiatric unit of a university hospital into five classes according to immediate circumstances. After a review of charts and interviews with patients and staff involved with each incident, assaults were classified as: injuries occurring during seclusion procedures (32 percent), assaults without provocation, even in retrospect (28 percent); assaults on peers after an argument or on staff members trying to break up patient arguments (20 percent); assaults on staff after denial of privileges, for example, smoking or leaving the ward (16 percent); and miscellaneous (4 percent).

Harris and Rice (1986) found that 38 percent of the assaults occurring at a large forensic facility, also the setting for Harris and Varney's (1986) report, occurred as a patient was being restrained. Examining workman's compensation forms, required after any incident that caused or could possibly cause staff injury, they found significantly more lost work days after incidents in which staff first made contact with a patient than in incidents in which patients first touched staff. Dietz and Rada (1983), also reporting on a forensic facility, also found that many injuries occurred as correction department officers restrained patients. They suggested that improved techniques could have a great impact on injury rates.

Timing, Location, Patient Density, and Structured Activity

Timing. A number of studies look at collections of incident reports grouped by time of occurrence to determine whether violence is more likely at certain times of the day. Time is linked to place and patient density because patients are usually in particular places at predetermined times. Place and time are also linked to ward activity because these are also usually prescheduled and routine.

Depp (1976) looked for temporal variations among violent incidents reported at St. Elizabeth's Hospital. Among the total patient population at St. Elizabeth's, about half carried the diagnosis of functional psychosis, 25 percent had organic brain syndrome, 5 percent were retarded, and the remaining 20 percent carried other diagnoses. Starting with the 379 officially reported incidents between November 1971 and July 1982, he narrowed his focus to 238, excluding from study incidents involving more than two people, incidents involving staff members, incidents that occurred off the ward, and incidents in which the victim retaliated. Depp found that between the hours of 6 A.M. and 10 P.M. the most significant increase in number of incidents occurred between 6 and 8 A.M. Two smaller increases occurred between 12 noon and 2 P.M. and between 4 and 6 P.M. Between 6 and 8 A.M. patients were required to rise, shower, dress, wash up, and eat breakfast. Patients also ate meals between 12 noon and 2 P.M. as well as between 4 and 6 P.M.

Pearson et al. (1986) studied violence among patients at a psychiatric hospital in the United Kingdom serving a semi-rural catchment area with three acute wards, six chronic wards, eight geriatric wards, and three special population wards. Of an average total census of 435, 30 percent were schizophrenic, 20 percent had affective illness, 33 percent had organic mental syndromes, and 15 percent carried other diagnoses. Investigators reviewed violent incident forms that were routinely completed by ward nursing staff. These were required whenever a patient intentionally damaged property or injured another person. It was discovered that incidents were "distributed fairly evenly throughout the morning, afternoon, and evening with very few at night. The hours in which violence peaked corresponded with the times when meals were served on the wards" (Pearson et al. 1986, p. 234). When nursing staff identified precipitants they most often mentioned arguments over food and personal space at meal times. However, different precipitants were most common when only events on the acute wards were considered.

Fottrell (1980) studied the temporal distribution of incidents of intentional physical violence, including self-injurious behavior, at three sites in the United Kingdom: Tooting Bec Psychiatric Hospital, Park Prewett Psychiatric Hospital, and the Chiltern Psychiatric Wing of Sutton General Hospital. Most incidents occurred at Tooting Bec, a facility in London. Diagnoses were not noted beyond a statement that patients of all kinds were treated except those who carried a primary diagnosis of mental retardation or those with a problem of serious chronic violence. To detect violent incidents, Fottrell used questionnaires completed by the ward sister or charge nurse. Senior nursing staff also visited wards daily to check for unreported incidents. Fottrell concluded that:

> Certain peak periods for violence were distinguishable at Tooting Bec where most incidents were recorded. The period between 7 A.M. and 9 A.M. when patients were getting up, washing, and breakfasting coincided with 30 percent of all incidents in the hospital. There was also a high incidence at meal times at Tooting Bec Hospital, and this was discernible at the two other hospitals, where, however, the total number of incidents was small. (Fottrell 1980, p. 221)

At the Chiltern Wing, a facility for short-term treatment of acute illness, 27 percent of all incidents occurred between 11 P.M. and 7 A.M. In contrast, only 7 percent of all incidents at Tooting Bec and 7 percent at Park Prewett occurred during these hours. This may be partly explained by the distribution of types of assaults at the different facilities. At the Chiltern Wing 35 percent of all assaults were self-directed, compared to 3 percent at Tooting Bec and 13 percent at Park Prewett.

Dietz and Rada (1982) studied the temporal distribution of a more narrowly defined group of incidents. They collected all seclusion reports from 1979 at a maximum security forensic facility. From this group they selected all incidents that described physical assaults. They excluded self-injury and any incident in which physical contact occurred only after staff intervention. All patients were male. Their chart diagnoses were not considered reliable but about 19 percent had no psychiatric disorder and about 75 percent carried diagnoses of schizophrenia, affective disorder, alcohol abuse, or antisocial personality disorder. Dietz and Rada found slight increases in the frequency of assault during mealtimes; these were 8 to 9 A.M., 11 A.M. to 12 P.M., and 4 to 5 P.M.

Quinsey and Varney (1977) studied 198 assaults occurring during a 1-year period at an all-male maximum security forensic hospital with different results. Of the patients, 44 percent were diagnosed as psychotic, 26 percent had a diagnosis of personality disorder, and 18 percent were mentally retarded. Assaultive incidents were identified by daily (Monday through Friday) review of the ward journal and daily interviews with ward staff and patients. Incidents were restricted to episodes of forceful physical contact between two or more people. Assault was most frequent not during mealtimes, but in the evening. At this time, patients watched television, mingled in the yard or corridor, and prepared for bed. There was also a sharp increase in frequency after breakfast, when patients mopped the floors or mingled without structured activities.

Harris and Varney (1986) studied assaults over a 10-year period at the same maximum security forensic hospital. Diagnoses were not noted. Ward reports were examined every day for reports of assault. *Assault* was defined as "patient initiated intentional physical contact of a forceful nature between two or more persons" (p. 178). If the ward report was ambiguous, patients, staff, and witnesses were interviewed whenever possible. The investigators concluded that, "just as reported by Quinsey and Varney, assaults occurred during periods of the day when patients mixed freely with each other in the absence of structured activity."

Location.   Dietz and Rada (1982) found that the probability that an incident was a physical assault rather than a verbal assault, self-injurious behavior, or disorderly conduct was related to location. Incidents were more likely to be physical assaults in dayrooms, on medication lines, in dining rooms, and in game rooms. These were areas of greatest social density, or patient-to-patient interactions, rather than simply physical density.

Harris and Varney (1986) also noted an association between location and assaults. Of the assaults, 59 percent occurred in the ward corridor, 19 percent occurred in the sunroom, 13 percent occurred in patients' rooms, 6 percent in the shower, and 3 percent in other locations. A greater percentage of assaults had occurred in patients' rooms in previous years (Quinsy and Varney 1977) before staff were discouraged from entering the rooms of patients who were agitated. Only a tiny fraction of assaults occurred in off-ward recreational and vocational training areas, although nearly all patients attended these activities. (It might be useful to know who did not attend and why.) This is consistent with Ekblom's (1970) assertion that violent incidents are more likely in the absence of therapeutic activity.

Patient density.   Patient density, in terms of average daily hospital census, was considered a possible correlate of assault by Kalogerakis (1971) in his study at Bellevue Psychiatric Hospital. He compared the number of assaultive incidents reported by nursing staff to the average daily census for each year between 1964 and 1969, but found no discernible relationship.

In summary, Depp (1976) and Fottrell (1980) found early-morning increases in incidents with less remarkable increases at midday and evening meals. Dietz and Rada (1982) and Pearson et al. (1986) found less marked, more uniform increases at each mealtime. Differences may be in part due to who is allowed in the dining room. At the institution Dietz and Rada (1982) studied, all patients but those in seclusion mingled in a dining room with their fellows from many different wards. They noted that, at other facilities (Quinsey and Varney 1977), disruptive, unstable patients are required to eat alone. This suggests that a small number of patients are responsible for a large proportion of assaults. Depp (1976) conjectured that early-morning hours are more associated with assault because at this time patients are confronted with the demands of staff and peers: to get out of bed, shower, dress appropriately, and repay food or cigarettes.

Cues

Most references in the literature to recognizable preludes to assaults, cues, are anecdotal. Marohn's (1982) discussion of violence on an adolescent inpatient unit stated that "rarely does violence occur in the hospital setting without the patient having signalled the likelihood in advance through either verbal or physical behavior" (p. 356). Adler et al.'s (1983) review contains a statement that verbal abuse usually escalates to violence. Arguments with relatives, sudden mood swings, and increasing demandingness are also suggested (Shraker et al. 1977) as preludes to assault, as are clenched fists, pacing, muscle tension, accelerated walking, yelling, throwing objects, curt speech, and irritability (Kronberg 1983).

Officers completing incident reports at Dietz and Rada's (1982) forensic facility were required to record a prelude to battery whenever possible. In 76.9 percent of 221 cases the battery was in progress or completed by the time officers were aware of an incident. Officers noted preludes, either through direct observation or reconstruction from accounts of combatants and witnesses, in only 23.1 percent of the incidents, 51 in all. Provocative talk preceded 12 of these 51 (23.5 percent), disobedience preceded 10 (19.6 percent), threats preceded 6 (11.8 percent), bizarre conduct preceded 5 (9.8 percent), provocative action preceded 5 (9.8 percent), throwing objects preceded 4 (7.8 percent), destroying property preceded 2 (3.9 percent), and being off limits preceded 1 (2.0 percent). Since all of these preludes were very common behaviors, they were considered poor predictors.

CONCLUSION

The usefulness of the papers reviewed is limited in a number of ways. It is limited by the type and quality of data reported. Case reports and anecdotal reviews are overly influenced by the personal opinions of the authors. If a violent incident is reported in a case report, it is probably atypical or unusual in some way, because, unfortunately, violence in psychiatric hospitals is common but case reports are not. A particular incident would have been chosen to illustrate a clinical impression but may not be representative. Many studies use data collected from incident reports. These are often incomplete records of incidents because staff may not be at the scene of an incident and so may never hear of it. Incident reports may be based on second-hand information. They may depend on the recollection of staff members, their powers of observation, and their hesitancy to incriminate, however obliquely, fellow staff members. Direct interviews with patients and staff have similar limitations.

Differences in methodologies make the studies cited difficult to compare. Studies vary greatly in their setting: state hospital vs. private hospital, general ward vs. specialized ward for especially disturbed patients, and so on. Patient populations studied vary greatly as well, with differences in age range, diagnostic mix, and degree of chronicity of illness. Differences in the definition and measurement of violent behavior are marked. Some investigators define violence broadly to include verbal assault and self-injurious behavior. Others are interested only in assaults on others that result in injuries. Violence may be measured through ward reports, special-incident reports, or personal interviews.

Ideally, prediction studies should consider interactions between specified state, trait, and situational variables. The environmental concomitants of assault on a private adolescent ward primarily treating characterologically disturbed youngsters should not be compared to those of assault on a long-term geriatrics ward with stabilized, nonpsychotic patients or to environmental concomitants of assault on a forensic ward with a mix of acutely psychotic and sociopathic patients.

Despite these limitations, this review points to a number of areas that deserve further investigation.

1. *The quality of ward rules and staff control as perceived by the patients.* Important factors seem to be staff confidence, consistency, firmness, and realistic expectations. The ability of staff to provide these may be impaired by poor morale. Staff need supportive leadership and cohesiveness in coping with feelings evoked by difficult patients and in enforcing ward policy.

The quality of limit setting is part of a broader entity: ward milieu. Although milieu research is difficult and contradictory, Vaglum et al. (1985), along with an excellent critique of existing work in the area, have identified milieu factors that seem to influence treatment outcome. Similar research should be undertaken to identify milieu factors that influence inpatient violence.

2. *The rewards of aggressiveness.* What happens after aggressive behavior may have an important impact on the future frequency of that behavior. Finding out just what happens every time requires close, constant observation with trained personnel. Different contingencies can have different effects on different patients. Despite these difficulties, experimenting with environmental manipulations after assaults occur could lead to safe, nonpharmacological treatments for individual patients and more rational, effective ward policies.

3. *Victim's behavior.* Assaults by psychiatric patients are often described as "apparently unprovoked" by ward staff. This may reflect the general public's view that the mentally ill may strike out suddenly, without cause or warning at any time. Several authors cited believe that assaults committed by psychiatric patients are frequently provoked, whether by intrusive and meddlesome patients (Depp 1983),

deliberately provocative patients (Branon 1948), or staff members who deny requests (Conn and Lion 1983) or attempt to restrain patients (Dietz and Rada 1983). Data on time of day seem to point to interpersonal provocations. The question of victim's provocation is quite difficult to resolve because assaults are infrequently observed as a whole, from inception to completion, or happen so quickly observers cannot be sure of what they saw. Beyond this question are several more. How do provokers provoke? What groups of patients tend to provoke? What is their state of mind (or type and degree of psychopathology) at the time?

Dietz and Rada's (1982) observation that assaults are more likely at mealtimes if unruly patients are not excluded from the dining room suggests that a few patients may be responsible for many assaults, as assaulters or perhaps as provokers.

4. *Ward activities.* Assaults are often said to occur during times of unstructured activities. What is it about structured activity that may prevent assaults? It may be that potentially disruptive patients are not allowed to participate. Assaults may also be deterred as a watchful occupational or recreational therapist spots cues and quickly intercedes. It would be useful to learn more about what happens during structured activities between patients and between patients and staff.

Our research group has in progress a project that can avoid many of the limitations of past research and investigate some of these questions (Brizer et al. 1988). We have installed closed-circuit television cameras in each corner of the dayroom on a special 14-bed treatment unit for violent patients. The unit is part of a large metropolitan state hospital serving primarily inner-city patients. It accepts no direct admissions, but only transfers from within the hospital. Patients transferred are considered unmanageably violent on their home wards as a result of repeated assaults on others, serious threats, or serious suicide attempts. While on the unit, patients spend most of their waking hours in the dayroom.

In a pilot study, taping took place 4 hours per day, usually 8 A.M. to 12 noon. From the original tapes, segments recording an assault plus the 5 preceding and 2 subsequent minutes of tape were transferred onto a separate tape for storage and review. A total of 129 hours of tape recorded over 35 weekdays were reviewed.

Early results indicate that this method of detecting assaults is considerably more sensitive than more traditional methods. We are currently involved in further characterizing the episodes in terms of specific behavioral antecedents, including victim's behavior, ward activities at the time of the assault, and consequences of the assault.

REFERENCES

Adler WN, Kreeger C, Ziegler P: Patient violence in a private psychiatric hospital, in Assaults Within Psychiatric Facilities. Edited by Lion JR, Reid WH. New York, Grune & Stratton, 1983

Azrin NH, Hake DF, Hutchinson RR: Elicitation of aggression by a physical blow. J Exp Anal Behav 8:55–57, 1965

Azrin NH, Hutchinson RR, Hake DF: Extinction-induced aggression. J Exp Anal Behav 9:191–204, 1966

Bandura A, Ross D, Ross S: Vicarious reinforcement and imitative learning. Journal of Abnormal and Social Psychology 67:601–607, 1963

Barker R, Dembo T, Lewin K: Frustration and aggression: an experiment with young children. University of Iowa Studies in Child Welfare 18: 1–314, 1941

Berkowitz L: Whatever happened to the frustration-aggression hypothesis? American Behavior Scientist 21:691–707, 1978

Branon AB: The social structure of a criminal unit of a psychiatric hospital. J Clin Psychopathol 9:128–135, 1948

Brizer DA, Crowner ML, Convit A, et al: Videotape recordings of inpatient assaults: a pilot study. Am J Psychiatry 145:751–752, 1988

Conn LM, Lion JR: Assaults in a university hospital, in Assaults Within Psychiatric Facilities. Edited by Lion JR, Reid WH. New York, Grune & Stratton, 1983

Depp FC: Violent behavior patterns on psychiatric wards. Aggressive Behavior 2:295–306, 1976

Depp FC: Assaults in a public mental hospital, in Assaults Within Psychiatric Facilities. Edited by Lion JR, Reid WH. New York, Grune & Stratton, 1983

Dietz DE, Rada RT: Battery incidents and batterers in a maximum security hospital. Arch Gen Psychiatry 39:31–34, 1982

Dietz DE, Rada RT: Interpersonal violence in forensic facilities, in Assaults Within Psychiatric Facilities. Edited by Lion JR, Reid WH. New York, Grune & Stratton, 1983

Erickson WD, Realmuto G: Frequency of seclusion in an adolescent psychiatric unit. J Clin Psychiatry 44:238–241, 1983

Esser AH: Interactional hierarchy and power structure on a psychiatric ward, in Behavior Studies in Psychiatry. Edited by Hutt SJ, Hutt C. Oxford, Pergamon Press, 1970

Felthous AR: Preventing assaults on a psychiatric inpatient ward. Hosp Community Psychiatry 35:1223–1226, 1984

Fottrell E: A study of violent behavior among patients in psychiatric hospital. Br J Psychiatry 136:216–221, 1980

Franzen MD, Lovell MR: Behavioral treatments of aggressive sequelae of brain injury. Psychiatric Annals 17:389–396, 1987

Gutheil TG, Rivinus TM: The cost of window breaking. Psychiatric Annals 7:47–51, 1977

Harris GT, Rice ME: Staff injuries sustained during altercation with psychiatric patients. Journal of Interpersonal Violence 1:193–211, 1986

Harris GT, Varney GW: A 10-year study of assaults and assaults on a maximum security psychiatric unit. Journal of Interpersonal Violence 1:173–191, 1986

Ionno JA: A prospective study of assaultive behavior in female psychiatric inpatients, in Assaults Within Psychiatric Facilities. Edited by Lion JR, Reid WH. New York, Grune & Stratton, 1983

Kalogerakis MG: The assaultive psychiatric patient. Psychiatr Q 45:372–381, 1971

Kronberg ME: Nursing interventions in the management of the assaultive patient, in Assaults Within Psychiatric Facilities. Edited by Lion JR, Reid WH. New York, Grune & Stratton, 1983

Levy P, Hartocolis P: Nursing aides and patient violence. Am J Psychiatry 133:429–431, 1976

Lion JR, Pasternak SA: Counter-transference reactions to violent patients. Am J Psychiatry 130:207–210, 1973

Lion JR, Madden DJ, Christopher RL: A violence clinic: three years' experience. Am J Psychiatry 133:432–434, 1976

Lorenz K: On aggression. London, Methuen, 1966

Marohn RC: Adolescent violence: causes and treatment. J Am Acad Child Psychiatry 4:354–360, 1982

Monahan J: The prediction of violent behavior: toward a second generation of theory and policy. Am J Psychiatry 141:10–15, 1984

Montagu A: The Nature of Human Aggression. New York, Oxford University Press, 1976

Patterson GR, Littman RA, Bricker W: Assertive behavior in children: a step toward a theory of aggression. Monogr Soc Res Child Dev 32:1–43, 1967

Pearson M, Wilmot E, Padi M: A study of violent behavior among inpatients in a psychiatric hospital. Br J Psychiatry 149:232–235, 1986

Quinsey VL, Varney GW: Characteristics of assaults and assaulters in a maximum security psychiatric unit. Crime and Justice 5:212–220, 1977

Schwarz CJ, Greenfield GP: Charging a patient with assault of a nurse on a psychiatric unit. Canadian Psychiatric Association Journal 23:197–200, 1978

Shaffer D, Meyer-Bahlburg HFL, Stockman CLJ: The development of aggression, in Scientific Foundations of Developmental Psychiatry. Edited by Rutter M. London, Heinemann, 1980

Stockman CLJ, Heiber P: Incidents in hospitalized forensic patients. Victimology 5:175–192, 1980

Straker M, Carmon P, Fulton J, et al: Assaultive behaviors in an institutional setting. Psychiatr J Univ Ottawa 2:185–190, 1977

Tardiff K: A survey of assault by chronic patients in a state hospital system, in Assaults Within Psychiatric Facilities. Edited by Lion JR, Reid WH. New York, Grune & Stratton, 1983

Vaglum P, Friis S, Karterud S: Why are the results of milieu therapy for schizophrenic patients contradictory? An analysis based on four empirical studies. Yale J Biol Med 58:349–361, 1985

Wong SE, Slama KM, Liberman RP: Behavioral analysis and therapy for aggressive psychiatric and developmentally disabled patients, in Clinical Treatment of the Violent Person. (Publication #85–1425) Edited by Roth LH. Washington, DC, US Department of Health and Human Services, 1985

Chapter 7

Child Abuse, Neglect, and Violent Criminal Behavior

Cathy Spatz Widom, Ph.D.

Chapter 7

Child Abuse, Neglect, and Violent Criminal Behavior

Although there is considerable uncertainty and debate about the extent of child abuse and neglect,[1] even less is known about their effects. In addition to the immediate consequences of child abuse or neglect that may involve physical injuries or psychological trauma, the emotional and developmental scars that accompany these children may persist. Because many other events in the child's life (e.g., natural abilities, physiological predispositions, social supports) may mediate the effects of child abuse and/or neglect, the long-term consequences are difficult to determine and remain unclear.

More than 20 years ago, in a brief clinical note entitled "Violence Breeds Violence—Perhaps?" Curtis (1963) discussed the battered child syndrome and expressed concern that these abused and neglected children would "become tomorrow's murderers and perpetrators of other crimes of violence, if they survive" (p. 386). By and large, the idea that violence begets violence is firmly established in the minds of professionals and the general public alike. In the words of Garbarino and Gilliam (1980),

> The premier developmental hypothesis in the field of abuse and neglect is, of course, the notion of intergenerational transmission, the idea that abusing parents were themselves abused as children and that neglect breeds neglect. (p. 111)

The idea is appealing; it makes intuitive sense. However, to para-

---

This chapter is based on a paper presented at the Society for Life History Research Conference on "Perinatal and Early Childhood Factors in Deviant Development" in Palm Springs, California, March 1986. The author thanks Deborah Stanley for her bibliographic assistance in the preparation of this review. Rolf Loeber, Joan McCord, and Robert Prentky provided valuable comments on an earlier draft.

123

phrase Garbarino and Gilliam, the alleged relationship between child abuse, neglect, and later violent behavior has not really "passed scientific muster" (p. 111).

The findings from a number of studies have suggested that child abuse is one possible factor contributing to the development of juvenile delinquency; however, none of these studies is conclusive. After reviewing this literature, Smith et al. (1979) concluded:

> [T]aken together they form a fairly consistent picture: that is, they point in the direction of a considerable link between abuse, neglect, and juvenile delinquency. (p. 129)

At the same time, these authors acknowledge that these "studies are not without their limitations" (p. 138).

According to Pagelow (1984), "The state of the art in child maltreatment is rudimentary and inconclusive" (p. 164). In a content analysis of approximately 3,000 abstracts listed in a National Center on Child Abuse and Neglect research bibliography, Bolton et al. (1981) found that only about 20 percent of all published works could be described as "research" and 84 percent of these were after-the-fact examinations of case records or aggregated statistics.

Furthermore, there are conflicting empirical reports. While a number of researchers suggest that aggression is a common outcome of abuse (e.g., Reidy 1977), other evidence suggests that withdrawal may be the result (Gutierres and Reich 1981). Some abused children may cope with the emotional stress by choosing to "identify with the aggressor" as their major behavioral pattern, whereas others may "identify with the victim" (Silver et al. 1969, p. 407).

This chapter examines the literature linking child abuse, neglect, and later delinquent and violent behavior, with the goal of assessing the strength of the assumed relationship. Excluded are medical reports that primarily describe proximal or distal physical sequellae of early childhood trauma (cf., Martin et al. 1974), as well as studies focusing on characteristics of abusing parents (cf., Spinetta and Rigler 1972).

To facilitate this review, the literature is divided into four general categories, drawing on the work of researchers from a number of different disciplines. The first type reflects primarily early reports of small numbers of abused children or violent/homicidal offenders in clinical contexts. The second category summarizes studies that examine the link between child abuse, neglect, and delinquency. The third focuses specifically on the relationship between abuse, neglect, and violent behavior. The final set of studies reviewed is drawn from the developmental psychology literature. Typically cross-sectional in design, these investigations describe levels of aggressiveness and social competence in abused and neglected children. Methodological problems are noted in the course of this review and then discussed more fully in a separate section. The chapter has a brief conclusion, stressing the critical need for further research. To this end, a number of questions are posed in hopes of stimulating and directing future research.

LITERATURE REVIEW

Reports of Small Numbers of Abused Children or Violent or Homicidal Offenders in Clinical Contexts

After the introduction of the battered child syndrome in the early 1960s, writers called attention to what they perceived to be the cycle of violence within the family (Curtis 1963). Attempts were made to locate and follow up children who had earlier been reported as abused. Friedman and Morse (1974) studied 41 cases 5 years later; Elmer (1967) studied 17 children 8 years later; Martin and Beezley (1977) studied 50 cases 4½ years later. In many of these reports, sample sizes were small, there were many lost cases, and the emphasis was on physical and intellectual consequences of abuse, with no special concern for aggressiveness or delinquency. Interestingly, a frequently cited study supporting the cycle of violence notion provides only modest support. In a follow-up study of 34 emergency room cases of suspected or proven child abuse (Silver et al. 1969), there was sufficient evidence in only 4 of these cases to show that the abuser had been abused as a child.

A number of reports are based on studies of murderers or violent individuals whose backgrounds were examined for evidence of childhood abuse. Several describe the family backgrounds of adolescents who attempted or succeeded in killing their parents (Duncan and Duncan 1971; Sorrells 1977; Tanay 1973). In one study of nine adolescent boys who had committed homicide as teenagers, King (1975) found that as children they were subjected to more beatings than their siblings. Sorrells (1977) noted that the families of his 31 youths charged with murder were "violent and chaotic." Bach-y-Rita and Veno (1974) reported that in 53 percent of their cases the parents of 62 habitually violent offenders engaged in physical combat between themselves.

More recently, working with FBI files, Ressler and Burgess (1985) examined the extent of abuse in a sample of sexual murderers. Of 31 murderers, 13 reported physical abuse in their childhood history, 23 reported psychological abuse, and 12 reported sexual abuse. Lewis et al. (1985) reported that 7 (78 percent) of their 9 young murderers (who had been evaluated prior to the murder) had experienced severe abuse by one or both parents, compared to about 60 percent of the nonviolent youths, although the difference was not significant.

While these small-scale clinical reports stimulate further research, their own statistical usefulness is limited. Thus researchers attempted to examine the consequences of early child abuse and neglect in the context of larger and more highly controlled investigations.

Studies Examining the Link Between Child Abuse, Neglect, and Delinquency

The second type of study addresses the relationship between child abuse, neglect, and delinquency, but does not address the question of violent behavior. These studies are summarized in Table 1. Of the three prospective studies in this group, each had design problems that detracted from the generalizability of the findings. Two of the three studies had no control group.

Alfaro's (1978) research involved 4,465 children and siblings referred to child protection agencies for suspected abuse or neglect in eight counties in New York State. Of these, 17.2 percent of the youths had had at least one subsequent contact with the juvenile court for delinquency or ungovernability. The strength of this study lies in its prospective design. Here the time order of the two factors—child abuse and delinquency—is clear. However, this strength is offset by the lack of a control group.

Gutierres and Reich (1981) studied a sample of 5,392 children who had been referred to the Arizona State Department of Economic Security for child abuse. Out of this group, 873 (16.2 percent) had subsequently been referred to juvenile court.

Control groups are critical here as with the Alfaro (1978) study because it is otherwise impossible to determine the percentage of youths *not* referred for child abuse who subsequently became delinquent or were referred to the juvenile court. Without control groups and thus some estimate of the base rate of occurrence of later delinquency in a similar group of nonabused youths, it is difficult to assess the meaningfulness of these findings.

As Newberger et al. (1983) pointed out in regard to Alfaro's (1978) research, but equally true of the Gutierres and Reich work,

Left open in the discussion, and unfortunately not susceptible to definitive analysis in this sample, is the extent to which the preferential selection of poor children both for reporting for maltreatment and for delinquency may have affected the perceived association and the extent to which poverty per se may have determined both problems. (p. 263)

The third prospective study, one by McCord (1983), is based on an analysis of 232 males who were divided into groups on the basis of parental treatment in childhood (abused, neglected, rejected, and loved[2]), as determined from case records that were originally written between 1939 and 1945. These men were then followed up between 1975 and 1979. Thus this study provides a 40-year perspective on the effects of child abuse and neglect.

McCord (1983) found that serious crimes (i.e., theft, auto theft, breaking and entering, burglary, or assault) were committed in childhood by half of the rejected children, about 20 percent of the abused and neglected children, and 11 percent of the loved children. In contrast, adult criminality seemed to have been less affected by parental rejection or abuse. McCord also noted that some of the males appeared to be relatively invulnerable to adverse effects from parental abuse and neglect: "Among the 97 neglected or abused children, had become criminal, alcoholic, mentally ill, or had died before reaching age 35, and 53 showed none of these signs of having been damaged" (p. 269).

While McCord's (1983) study is the most methodologically sound of the ones discussed, her sample sizes were relatively small. There is also some question about the severity of the abuse and neglect, given post-hoc imposition of criteria for inclusion in the abused and neglected categories.

Most of the studies in Table 1 identify a sample of delinquent youths, and utilize a reverse records check to determine the incidence of abuse or neglect in the delinquents' backgrounds. For example, Lewis and Shanok (1977) checked the hospital records of 109 delinquents and 109 nondelinquents (matched for age, sex, race, and socioeconomic status) to determine the relationship between delinquency and abuse. Approximately 9 percent of the delinquents, in contrast to only 1 percent of the nondelinquents, had been seen at the hospital for services specifically related to child abuse.

These retrospective studies, in particular, face threats to validity in terms of inaccuracies in recording and other biases. Only two of the studies that retrospectively checked records used control groups (Glueck and Glueck 1950; Lewis and Shanok 1977). Without such comparisons, it is difficult to assess the external validity of the findings.

Many of these studies represent after-the-fact analyses of preexisting records or depend on the retrospective recall of the subjects for information. For example, Kratcoski (1982) abstracted information about abuse experiences by reading case summaries written by psychologists or social workers. These findings may be distorted because in many of the files the psychologists or social workers who

Table 1. Child abuse, neglect, and delinquent behavior

Study	Subjects	Criterion for abuse and/or neglect	Findings
Prospective			
Alfaro (1978)	All cases referred to public and private protection agencies in 1952–1953 ($n = 4,465$)	Referral to child protection agencies	17.2% (740) had had at least one subsequent contact with juvenile court for delinquency over 15-year period
Gutierres and Reich (1981)	5,392 children referred to Ariz. State Dept. Econ. Sec., Child Protective Services	Referral for physical, emotional, or sexual abuse	16.2% (873) had been referred to juvenile court
McCord (1983)	201 males orig. studied in 1939–1945; retraced in 1975 and 1979: 48 neglected; 49 abused; 34 rejected; 101 loved	Childhood abuse, neglect, or rejection	Rejected children (29%) had significantly higher rates of juvenile delinquency than loved children (7%); abused (10%) and neglected (15%) were in between
Retrospective			
Glueck and Glueck (1950)	500 delinquents in juvenile institutions, 500 nondelinquents (matched for age, race, IQ, and neighborhood)	Families needed help from service agencies for abuse or neglect of children	86% delinquent families need help vs. 44% nondelinquent families
Lewis & Shanok (1977)	109 delinquents 109 nondelinquents (matched on age, sex, race, and socioeconomic status)	Hospital use because of abuse	8.6% delinquents used hospital services versus 1% controls

Table 1. Child abuse, neglect, and delinquent behavior (*continued*)

Study	Subjects	Criterion for abuse and/or neglect	Findings
Alfaro (1978)	All cases referred to problem intake depts. and juvenile courts in NY state 1971–1972 (*n*=1963)	Prior contact with child protection agencies	22.8% had prior contact
Wick (n.d.)	50 male youths referred to Central Texas Youth Service Bureau	Self-reported abuse and neglect	29% had abuse or neglect in their backgrounds
Mouzakitis (n.d.)	60 female delinquents committed to Ark. State Training School for Girls (Feb 1977)	Self-reported childhood discipline by physical means	86% reported on questionnaire discipline by physical means: 13% hands only, 23% hands and belts, 50% objects and hands
Kratcoski (1982)	863 case files of delinquent youths incarcerated in four Ohio institutions for serious male offenders	Physical abuse or neglect in case files	25.8% (223) had experienced some form of physical abuse or neglect

interviewed the youths never brought up issues about parent relationships, missing the chance to uncover possible abuse. Furthermore, the parents had rarely been officially charged with child abuse, and in some instances, determinations about whether child abuse had occurred had to be made by the researchers, as was the case in the McCord (1983) study.

Although there appears to be some relationship between early child abuse and neglect and later delinquent behavior, conclusions remain tentative due to serious methodological limitations. In studies using a retrospective design, estimates of abuse in the backgrounds of delinquents typically range from 8 to 26 percent. Using a prospective design, delinquency in children who had been abused or neglected occurred in less than 20 percent of the cases. In the case of the McCord (1983) study, rejected children had the highest rates of recorded delinquency.

Studies Examining the Link Between Child Abuse, Neglect, and Violent Behavior

The third set of studies specifically addresses the relationship between abuse, neglect, and violent behavior (see Table 2). The majority of these studies utilized a cross-sectional design and divided delinquents or psychiatric patients into subgroups.

The most common design utilized delinquents who were then divided into more specialized groups: abused and nonabused (Alfaro, 1978; Bolton et al. 1977; Geller and Ford-Somma 1984; Kratcoski 1982), socialized and unsocialized aggressives (Jenkins 1968), and violent and nonviolent (Hartstone and Hansen 1984; Lewis et al. 1979). In each of these studies, the author(s) related differences between delinquent subgroups to their propensity to engage in violent behavior or their experiencing or witnessing of child abuse.

A number of these studies provide some support for a relationship between early abuse and later violent behavior. Unsocialized aggressive children were more likely to come from rejecting and physically punishing families, whereas the families of nonaggressive, socialized children were more often "neglectful" (Jenkins 1968). More violent boys were more likely to have experienced abuse or witnessed extreme physical abuse than nonviolent boys (Lewis et al. 1979). Of 114 violent youth from four states, 15 percent had suffered from child abuse; 2 percent had been sexually victimized in the home (Hartstone and Hansen 1984). The more abuse reported by incarcerated juvenile offenders, the more violent crimes they committed and the more they engaged in violence for its own sake (Geller and Ford-Somma 1984).

On the other hand, several studies offer contradictory evidence. Although more than three-quarters of the youths in both groups had committed at least one act that would be considered violent (Kratcoski 1982), the abused delinquents were *not* more violent than nonabused delinquents. In the large sample of abused and nonabused delinquents studied by Alfaro (1978), only slightly more of the abused delinquents (25.8%) committed crimes involving violence than the nonabused delinquents (21.3%). Bolton et al. (1977) reported that abused youths were *less* likely to engage in "aggressive" crimes (disturbing the peace, fighting, assault, assault with a deadly weapon, aggravated assault and battery, armed robbery, and strong armed robbery), but were more likely to be arrested for "escape" crimes (truancy, runaway, or missing juvenile).

In some studies, groups of psychiatric patients were compared. Climent and Ervin (1972) studied 40 violent emergency room patients. These violent patients were more likely to have been beaten as children than a group of nonviolent subjects, with more frequent physical assaults by both mothers and fathers reported. Records of assaultive and nonassaultive adolescent male hospital patients (Blount and Chandler 1979) were reviewed to determine evidence of prior abuse. Assaultive patients had a higher incidence of prior abuse (8 out of 15, or 53 percent) than nonassaultive patients (3 out of 15, or 20 percent).

In a sample of delinquents referred to a psychiatric clinic, Tarter et al. (1984) found that those who were abused were more likely to commit violent offenses than those who were not abused. In another study, an unselected sample of children and adolescents receiving psychiatric services at a large city hospital in 1 year were divided into abused[3] and nonabused groups and their violent behavior was compared (Monane et al. 1984). Overall, there was a high incidence of physical abuse (42 percent) in the medical histories of these patients, although the most significant factor distinguishing the abused from nonabused psychiatrically hospitalized children and adolescents was violence. Among the abused patients, 72 percent had been extremely violent, compared with only 46 percent of the nonabused patients. Homicidal behavior was slightly more common in the abused group (35 percent) than in the nonabused (24 percent) group.

Most of the studies in Table 2 suffer from methodological problems. A number are composed of very small samples (Blount and Chandler 1979; Lewis et al. 1985; Ressler and Burgess 1985; Sorrells 1977). With few exceptions, the studies are of youths and adolescents and, therefore, cannot address the possible long-term consequences of abuse and neglect into adulthood. *All* lack a normal (i.e., non-

Table 2. Child abuse, neglect, and violent behavior

Study	Subjects	Outcome measure	Findings
Delinquents			
Jenkins (1968)	445 unsocialized, aggressive, assaultive delinquents and 231 socialized delinquents	Aggression and assaultive vs. property crimes	Assaultive: families were punitive, rejecting, used extreme forms of physical punishment. Property crime delinquents: families were poorer, larger, and neglectful
Alfaro (1978)	Delinquents from 1970s sample divided into two groups: abused/neglected and non-abused/neglected	Commit violent crimes	Of abused/neglected, 25.8% committed violent crimes. Of nonabused/neglected, 21.3% committed crimes involving violence
Lewis et al. (1979)	97 incarcerated boys divided into extremely and less violent groups	Violent behavior	More violent boys were more likely to have experienced or witnessed extreme physical abuse than less violent boys
Bolton et al. (1981)	Of 5,392 children referred to Ariz. State Dept. Econ. Sec., Child Protection Services: 783 in juvenile court; siblings; 900 reported juvenile offenders; siblings	Escape and aggressive crimes	Crimes (%) Escape Aggressive Abused 40.3 3.4 Siblings 29.1 6.1 Control 17.7 5.4 Siblings 12.1 5.3
Kratcoski (1982)	863 incarcerated delinquent youths divided into abused and nonabused groups	Violent delinquent behavior	Abused delinquents were *not* more violent than nonabused delinquents

Table 2. Child abuse, neglect, and violent behavior *(continued)*

Study	Subjects	Outcome measure	Findings
Geller and Ford-Somma (1984)	223 juvenile offenders in NJ training schools	Arrests for violent crimes	The more that offenders were abused, the more violent crimes they committed and the more they engaged in violence for its own sake (multiple regression analysis)
Hartstone and Hansen (1984)	114 violent youths in 4 states who met legal definition of "violent offender" over 14-month period	Violent offender conviction	15% of study youths had suffered from child abuse; 2% had been sexually victimized in the home
Patients			
Blount and Chandler (1979)	30 randomly selected male adolescent state hospital patients: 15 admitted for assault; 15 no evidence assault behavior	Assaultive behavior outside and within hospital	Assaultive patients: 8/15 prior abuse Nonassaultive patients: 3/15 prior abuse
Tarter et al. (1984)	101 delinquent adolescents referred consecutively to psychiatric institutions & clinic: 27 abused, 74 nonabused	Commit violent offenses	Delinquents who were abused were more likely to commit violent offenses than those who were not abused (44% vs. 16%)
Monane et al. (1984)	Unselected sample of 166 children and adolescents admitted to psychiatric service of large city hospital in 1 year, divided into abused & nonabused groups	Violent behavior rating (4-point scale)	72% of abused had been extremely violent, as compared with 42% of nonabused

delinquent or nonpsychiatric patient) control group. Without appropriate control groups, it is once again difficult to assess the meaningfulness of these findings.

Studies of Abuse, Neglect, and Aggressive Behavior in Young Children

The final set of studies focuses on the relationship between abuse, neglect, and aggressive behavior in young children. Drawn primarily from experimental and laboratory studies, this research is summarized in Table 3. Given that the emphasis here is on the child's behavior, only those reports that present findings for children are included. Excluded, then, are studies of parent-child interactions where the report includes no separate analysis of the child's behavior.

As can be seen, age groups vary, as do definitions of child abuse and neglect. A variety of outcome measures are used: videotapes and direct observations of social interaction in the home or day-care settings, levels of aggression as reflected in projective tests (Thematic Apperception Test stories) or in free play environments, or case worker reports. However, the results indicate with some consistency that the abused children manifested more aggressive and problematic behavior, even at these early ages. These studies also illustrate the importance of distinguishing between early experiences of abuse and neglect when examining later outcomes.

Most of the earlier studies failed to separate abused and neglected children into distinct groups. However, the findings of Bousha and Twentyman (1984) and Hoffman-Plotkin and Twentyman (1984) reinforce the importance of treating the groups separately. Abused and neglected children showed greater amounts of physical and verbal aggression than did control children. The abused children, although not the neglected children, also differed from controls on vocal-negative behavior and noncompliance. On the other hand, neglected children displayed a depressed rate of positive social behavior, less verbal and nonverbal instruction, and fewer social initiations than other children. "These data imply that abuse and neglect represent fundamentally different forms of child maltreatment and that combining maltreating groups, as has frequently been done, may actually obscure the important differences" (Bousha and Twentyman 1984, p. 113).

By and large, these studies have control groups. Control children are typically well matched with abused children for age, sex, race, and often socioeconomic status and other relevant parental background characteristics (Friedrich and Wheeler 1982). Thus these studies do not suffer from the same methodological problems as

Table 3. Abuse, neglect, and aggressive behavior in children

Study	Subjects	Design Comments	Outcome Measures	Findings
Martin and Beezley (1977)	50 abused children (mean age, 6 yr 5 mo)	Assessed 4½ yr after physical abuse first identified	Observations of 9 characteristics from physical and neuro-development exam, IQ testing, and interviews	Frequency of characteristic: impaired ability for enjoyment 33; behavioral symptoms 31; low self-esteem 26; withdrawal 12; opposition 12; hypervigilance 11; compulsivity 11; precocious behavior 10; school learning problems 9
Reidy (1977)	20 abused children (A), 16 nonabused-neglected (NA), 22 normal children (N) (ages 6–7 years)	Cross-sectional	Aggressive characteristics: aggressive fantasies (TAT) and observation of aggressive behavior in free-play and school settings	TAT: $A > NA$ and N; Freeplay: $A > NA$ and N; School: A and $NA > N$
George and Main (1979)	10 abused toddlers, 10 matched toddlers from families experiencing stress (age 1–3 yr)	Observations during social interactions in daycare settings	Social interactions: approach, avoidance, and aggression	Abused infants more frequently physically assaulted peers; harassed caregivers verbally and nonverbally; assaulted or threatened to assault caregivers; avoided other children; were less likely to approach caregivers in response to friendly gestures

Table 3. Abuse, neglect, and aggressive behavior in children (*continued*)

Study	Subjects	Design Comments	Outcome Measures	Findings
Kinard (1980)	30 abused vs. 30 nonabused children (matched for age, sex, race, welfare status, birth order, parent structure, and residence), 5–12 yr	Psychological testing 1 year after incident	Psychological tests measuring: self-concept, aggression, socialization with peers, establishment of trust in people, separation from mother	Abused children differed in all 5 areas of emotional development: more neglective self-concepts and handling of aggressive impulses in more aggressive way than nonabused children
Baird (1982)	63 physically abused, 96 neglected, 34 noninvolved sibs	Cross-sectional; child protective service caseworkers completed checklists	Aggressiveness; antisocial behavior; cognitive deficits; psychopathology	Differences among children due to strong effects for sex, and associated family problems
Wasserman et al. (1983)	12 abused infant and mother pairs, 12 control infant and mother pairs (matched for age, sex, and race), mean age, 14 mo	Cross-sectional; videotaping during free-play situation	Measures of cognitive and social competence	Abused infants' scores lower on Bayley Mental Development scale than controls; abused infants were more likely to ignore or refuse maternal distractions than controls, but not less likely to comply with orders.

Table 3. Abuse, neglect, and aggressive behavior in children (*continued*)

Study	Subjects	Design Comments	Outcome Measures	Findings
Bousha and Twentyman (1984)	12 abused child-mother pairs (A), 12 neglected child-mother pairs (N), 12 control child-mother pairs (C) mean age, 4 yr	Naturalistic observation in home for 3 consecutive days for 90 min/day	Raters' coding of interactions of mother and child	A and N children showed: fewer positive behaviors such as verbal and nonverbal affection and play behavior; more aggressive behavior such as physical, verbal, and vocal aggression. N children differed from others in demonstrating less verbal and nonverbal instruction and fewer social interactions
Herrenkohl et al. (1984)	182 parent-child interactions with maltreated children; 58 interactions of control families (chosen from child welfare agencies, daycare programs, Head Start, etc.) (mean age, 50 mo)	Parent-child observations in the home in the context of play sessions	Child behaviors coded during observation as well as observer ratings of 5 dimensions: nervousness, warmth, aggression, and global rating	Neglected children showed more talking to observers, but did not differ on other ratings; abused children (harsh discipline) talked more to observers and global ratings of interactions were more negative; neglected and harsh discipline children did less speaking than control group, showed less task involvement, and had more negative global ratings of interactions, and less warmth in the opinion of observers

those summarized in Tables 1 and 2. Definitions of abuse and neglect are generally more careful, cases of abuse and neglect are typically substantiated and validated, and there is little dependence on retrospective data. However, these studies usually are carried out concurrently while parents are in some form of therapy or parent group. In few studies (Kinard 1980; Martin and Beezley 1977) did the abuse or neglect occur during some substantial time period prior to the assessment or laboratory testing.

METHODOLOGICAL CONSIDERATIONS

Over the last several years, scholarly reviews of the literature on child abuse have criticized existing research as methodologically flawed and limited in its generalizability, scientific validity, and, ultimately, its policy relevance (e.g., Berger 1980; Newberger et al. 1983). A number of major limitations characterizing studies linking early child abuse, neglect, and delinquent or violent behavior are highlighted here.

One major problem is the *lack of specificity in defining predictor and outcome criteria*. Criteria for defining the phenomena—child abuse or neglect—are often imprecise and vary widely, including unsubstantiated cases. Child abuse can be limited to a clinical condition (broken bones or severe physical trauma) or it can refer to a wider range of activities that may include failure to provide adequate food or clothing or improper care for the child (Young 1964). Basic differences in the definitions or criteria for abuse or neglect affect not only estimates of its frequency, but also the replicability of assessment. As we have seen, most studies fail to distinguish between abused and neglected children, treating them as one group.

In terms of *outcome variables*, most studies relate early child abuse and neglect to generalized delinquent behavior, and depend on juvenile court records exclusively. Little of this research focuses on violent criminal behavior. When violent behaviors are examined, the criteria range from evidence of assaultive and aggressive behaviors to convictions for violent offenses. Most studies do not address the long-term consequences of early abuse and neglect, and few have traced the effects of abuse or neglect through adulthood (or adult court records). Blind assessments of outcomes are made only rarely.

Research in this area is also characterized by a general *failure to consider statistical base rates and lack of appropriate comparison or control groups*. As Monahan (1981) so convincingly argued, one of the most important single pieces of information we can have in the prediction of violence is the base rate for violent behavior in the population with which we are dealing. Particularly in the area of abuse and neglect, there is a tendency to place too much emphasis on individual case information at the expense of base rates. Webster (1977) published base rates for violent crime for the U.S. population, illustrating that different subgroups have different base rates of arrests for violent behavior. Males were arrested for violent crimes nine times more frequently than females, blacks more often than whites, and people in urban areas more often than in the suburbs. In determining whether the specific early childhood experiences of abuse or neglect lead to later violent behavior, base rates—from the same population of people at the same time period—must be taken into account.

A number of researchers have argued that official reports of child abuse overrepresent low-income families (e.g., Newberger et al. 1977). This represents a serious concern since it is clear that abuse and neglect occur in all social classes. However, national surveys of family violence have found that those with the lowest incomes are more likely to abuse their children (Straus et al. 1980). Phrased somewhat differently, low socioeconomic status characterizes the largest portion of abuse families (Pelton 1978).

Even without the additional presence of undernutrition, maternal deprivation, parental unemployment, parental alcoholism or drug problems, or inadequate social and family functioning that often coexist with abuse or neglect, a home environment in which abuse or neglect takes place influences the development of the child. Inasmuch as these characteristics frequently occur in abusive or neglectful environments, control groups matched on socioeconomic status and other relevant variables become vital components of this research.

Appropriate control groups are also important for another reason. Because many of these same family and demographic characteristics relate to delinquency and later criminality (Loeber and Dishion 1983), control groups are necessary to assess the independent effects of abuse or neglect. Without control groups to provide a rough estimate of such abuse rates, it is difficult to assess the magnitude of relationships.

Much of the research linking abuse and neglect and delinquency or violent behavior is also based on designs weakened by *questionable accuracy of information due to the retrospective nature* of survey research data or reliance on second-hand information (e.g., parental reports), rather than on directly observed or validated behaviors.

Retrospective data are notoriously unreliable (Yarrow et al. 1970). There is evidence that descriptions of the incidence of certain phenomena differ depending on whether self-reports are made in the context of retrospective or prospective studies (Koeske 1981; Sommer 1978). The term *retrospective recall bias* emphasizes the risk of distortion and loss of information from recalling events from a prior time period.

If events are recalled after a period of years, events and conditions are seen and described in the context of later circumstances and one's present situation, from which they take much of their meaning and significance. Respondents might "forget" or redefine their behavior in accordance with their current situation. There is a tendency for much child abuse research to be based on self-reports by parents (typically mothers) who are participating (voluntarily or involuntarily) in groups for abusing parents. It would not be surprising to find social desirability factors influencing someone to report their behavior in more favorable terms. Similarly, defendants charged with serious crimes might believe they would benefit from special leniency or increased empathy from others by claiming early child abuse or severe childhood neglect.

Another problem we have seen is the use of *weak sampling techniques* involving opportunity or convenience samples, data gathered from cases that medical or psychiatric practitioners have at hand, or anecdotal clinical accounts or small-scale case studies. These provide valuable clinical insights and hypotheses to direct and stimulate further research but their usefulness in statistical terms is limited.

A related concern is the *ex-post-facto nature of most of the studies*, which offers little predictive power. This is particularly problematic if the design involves a reverse records check, starting with groups who have previously been labeled delinquent. Although a reasonable place to begin inquiries in new areas of research, correlational studies rarely address etiology or causality.

DISCUSSION

More than 20 years after Curtis (1963) questioned the intergenerational transmission of violence, and despite the fact that a number of authors have documented the immediate physical or emotional sequellae of severe abuse and neglect, we still do not have a clear picture of the long-term consequences of these early childhood experiences. The current state of our knowledge concerning the link between child abuse, neglect, and delinquent or adult violent criminal behavior is based on weak and inconsistent findings. Most of the studies are flawed by serious methodological, definitional, and conceptual problems. What conclusions can we draw?

First, there is some evidence that a relationship exists between early child abuse, neglect, and delinquency. Between 15 and 20 percent of delinquent youths appear to have had child abuse or neglect in their backgrounds.

Second, recent cross-sectional work in developmental psychology indicates that early child abuse *and* neglect are related to aggressive behavior in children as young as infants and toddlers. These studies also demonstrate the need to consider the experience of neglect as distinct from abuse. Neglected children are not the same, conceptually or empirically, as abused children. With one exception (McCord 1983), most of the large-scale studies examining the relationship between abuse and neglect and delinquent or violent behavior have included both abused and neglected children. Only the laboratory studies have systematically examined and reported differences between separate samples of abused and neglected children. It may, in fact, be that neglected children show *higher* levels of subsequent violent behavior than those who are abused. Combining the abused and neglected groups or studying only abused children may obscure important behavioral outcomes.

Third, there is little convincing evidence that these early childhood experiences have lasting consequences for the commission of serious violent crimes in adulthood. While a number of researchers have suggested that aggression is a common outcome, other evidence indicates that withdrawal may also be related to early abusive experiences. Most of the existing work in this area examines delinquent behavior; few studies focus specifically on *adult* violent criminal behavior. Of the studies examining violent behavior, findings are contradictory: some found more violent offenses committed by abused delinquents; others found no differences between abused and non-abused delinquents. In most of the studies reviewed, the majority of abused children became neither delinquent nor violent offenders.

Having examined the findings of existing research, what directions should future research take?

FUTURE RESEARCH

Future research must examine the general relationship between early childhood experiences of abuse and neglect and later violent criminal behavior, and must overcome as much as possible the methodological shortcomings of previous research. Existing research provides very little information about the extent to which the type of abuse or neglect, the duration, or the age at which it occurs is related to later outcome. We know very little about whether sexual and physical abuse affects children in the same way, whether the effect of one is more serious than the other, or whether males and females react differently to abuse and neglect. Several broad sets of questions follow that are illustrative but by no means exhaustive of possible directions for future research.

Is there a significant and meaningful relationship between early child abuse and/or neglect and later violent criminal behavior? Are both abuse and neglect associated with later violent criminal behavior or is only one? Are abuse and/or neglect related to particular forms of violent behavior? Do the long-term effects of abuse and/or neglect occur only in the context of specific family patterns or demographic characteristics?

Kinard (1980), Rolston (1971), and Sears et al. (1957) have suggested that the older the child when the abuse occurred, the less likely the child would be to exhibit aggressive behavior. Does the relationship between child abuse, neglect, and violent behavior vary depending on the age at which the abuse or neglect occurs? Is there a critical time period before or after which the effects of these early experiences are magnified or minimized? Are the long-term consequences more severe if the abuse or neglect occurs before a certain age or are the consequences similar, regardless of the age at which it occurs?

Is there a relationship between child abuse, neglect, and later violent behavior in males *and* females? Or, does the outcome differ depending on the sex of the child? Pagelow (1984) noted that "whenever reports are characterized by sex, they show that there is a much stronger and consistent association between boys who witness or are subjected to violence and later adult violent behavior than is true for girls" (p. 253). If sex differences exist, do they parallel sex differences in socialization experiences—reflecting perhaps a basic gender difference in respect to the expression of aggression?

Furthermore, males and females may suffer from different forms of abuse. Not surprisingly, of the 5,392 children who had been referred for child abuse, Gutierres and Reich (1981) found that the sample of sexually abused juveniles was overwhelmingly female. Similarly, Adams-Tucker (1982) found girls to be more sexually victimized than boys—by a greater number of molesters (more often fathers and other adult men), by more types of molestation, and over longer periods of time.

Is violent criminal behavior linked only to certain *types of abuse* or does abuse generally lead to these consequences? Are the consequences of one form of abuse more destructive and long lasting than other types?

Is early sexual abuse an antecedent to later sex crimes? Finkelhor and Browne (1985) suggested that some children who have been victimized, especially adolescent boys but sometimes even younger children, become sexually aggressive and victimize their peers or younger children. While numerous articles and books have been written about sexual child abuse as an antecedent to prostitution in females, until recently very little was written about male victims of sexual abuse. Most of these reports are based on psychiatric case materials from offenders who were arrested or treated because of their offense. What are the long-term consequences of early sexual victimization in males?

What is the relationship, if any, between the duration of abuse and/or neglect and violent criminal behavior? One beating, or one act of violence, is probably not enough to turn a child into a delinquent. But this is an issue that has not received sufficient attention.

Does the perpetrator of the abuse (whether it is parent, stepparent, family friend, stranger, etc.) make a difference in terms of the link to later violent criminal behavior? In her study of the proximal effects of sexual abuse, Adams-Tucker (1982) found that the children molested by their fathers appeared to suffer more than the other children. Do the long-term consequences also differ?

Finally, not all children who grow up in violent homes become violent adults. In McCord's (1983) study, some of the men appeared to be relatively invulnerable to the adverse effects of parental abuse and neglect. Certainly, there are a wide variety of environmental stresses and potential triggering mechanisms, and many other factors are involved in the learning process. Can we identify life events that act as buffers to prevent the long-term consequences of these negative early childhood experiences?

Perhaps our conceptualization of the relationship between violence and child abuse has been overly simplistic. Curtis (1963) recognized the unlikely possibility that there would be a simple causal relationship between early child abuse and later crimes of violence:

> Important psychological differences probably underline, for example, the murder of an unfaithful lover and murder associated with armed robbery, murders which are and are not concealed, etc. . . . The child's reaction and adaptation to abuse probably vary with many other aspects of his life and circumstances. (p. 387)

NOTES

1. Estimates of the number of child abuse and neglect cases in the United States range from approximately 500,000 per year (Burgdorf 1980; Gil 1970; Light 1974; Zalba 1971) to as high as 2.3 million (Straus et al. 1980). In terms of incidence rates, it has been estimated that 10.5 of 1,000 children under age 18 in the United States are abused and/or neglected annually.

2. Men who had been subjected to consistently punitive, physical punishments were classified as *abused*. Those whose parents interacted with them infrequently, showing neither affection nor rejection, were classified as *neglected*. Among those not abused, the ones who had at least one parent who seemed concerned for the child's welfare and generally pleased with his behavior were classified as *loved*. The remaining group, those neither abused nor neglected but also not loved, were classified as *rejected* (McCord 1983).

3. Abuse was defined as "deliberate aggressive acts by family members or others outside the home that caused or could have been expected to cause serious injury (e.g., hit with a wooden board, thrown down a flight of stairs). Ordinary spankings or beatings on the buttocks with a strap or switch were not considered abuse" (Monane et al. 1984, p. 654).

REFERENCES

Adams-Tucker C: Proximate effects of sexual abuse in childhood: a report on 28 children. Am J Psychiatry 139:1252–1256, 1982

Alfaro J: Child Abuse and Subsequent Delinquent Behavior. New York, Select Committee on Child Abuse, 1978

Bach-y-Rita G, Veno A: Habitual violence: a profile of 62 men. Am J Psychiatry 131:1015–1017, 1974

Baird DA: A Comparative Study of Abused and Neglected Children and Their Siblings. Dissertation Abstracts International 43:1276-B (#DA82-18998), 1982

Berger AM: The child abusing family, I: methodological issues and parent-related characteristics of abusing families. American Journal of Family Therapy 8:53–66, 1980

Blount HR, Chandler TA: Relationship between childhood abuse and assaultive behavior in adolescent male psychiatric patients. Psychol Reports 44:1126, 1979

Bolton FG, Reich J, Gutierres SE: Delinquency patterns in maltreated children and siblings. Victimology 2:349–359, 1977

Bolton FG, Reich J, Gutierres SE: The 'study' of child maltreatment: when is research . . . research? Journal of Family Issues 2:531–541, 1981

Bousha DM, Twentyman CT: Mother-child interactional style in abuse, neglect, and control groups: naturalistic observations in the home. J Abnorm Psychol 93:106–114, 1984

Burgdorf K: Recognition and Reporting of Child Maltreatment. Rockville, Md, Westat, 1980

Climent CE, Ervin FR: Historical data in the evaluation of violent subjects: a hypothesis generating study. Am J Psychiatry 27:621–624, 1972

Curtis GC: Violence breeds violence—perhaps? Am J Psychiatry 120:386–387, 1963

Duncan JW, Duncan GM: Murder in the family: a study of some homicidal adolescents. Am J Psychiatry 127:74–79, 1971

Elmer E: Children in Jeopardy: A Study of Abused Minors and Their Families. Pittsburgh, University of Pittsburgh Press, 1967

Finkelhor D, Browne A: The traumatic impact of child sexual abuse: a conceptualization. Am J Orthopsychiatry 55:530–541, 1985

Friedman S, Morse CW: Child abuse: a five-year follow-up of early case findings in the emergency department. Pediatrics 54:404–410, 1974

Friedrich WH, Wheeler KK: The abusing parent revisited: a decade of psychological research. J Nerv Ment Dis 170:577–588, 1982

Garbarino J, Gilliam G: Understanding Abusive Families. Lexington, Mass, Lexington Books, 1980

Geller M, Ford-Somma L: Violent Homes, Violent Children. A Study of Violence in the Families of Juvenile Offenders. (New Jersey State Department of Corrections, Trenton. Division of Juvenile Services.) Washington, DC, National Center on Child Abuse and Neglect, 1984

George C, Main M: Social interactions of young abused children: approach, avoidance, and aggression. Child Dev 50:306–318, 1979

Gil D: Violence Against Children: Physical Child Abuse in the United States. Cambridge, Mass, Harvard University Press, 1970

Glueck S, Glueck E: Unraveling Juvenile Delinquency. Cambridge, UK, Cambridge University Press, 1950

Gutierres S, Reich JA: A developmental perspective on runaway behavior: its relationship to child abuse. Child Welfare 60:89–94, 1981

Hartstone E, Hansen KV: The violent juvenile offender: an empirical portrait, in Violent Juvenile Offenders: An Anthology. Edited by Mathias RA. San Francisco, National Council on Crime and Delinquency, 1984

Herrenkohl EC, Herrenkohl RC, Toedter L, et al: Parent-child interactions in abusive and nonabusive families. J Am Acad Child Psychiatry 23:641–648, 1984

Hoffman-Plotkin D, Twentyman C: A multimodel assessment of behavioral and cognitive deficits in abused and neglected preschoolers. Child Dev 55:794–802, 1984

Jenkins RL: The varieties of adolescent's behavior problems and family dynamics. Am J Psychiatry 124:1440–1445, 1968

Kinard EM: Emotional development in physically abused children. Am J Orthopsychiatry 50:686–696, 1980

King CH: The ego and the integration of violence in homicidal youth. Am J Orthopsychiatry 45:134–145, 1975

Koeske RD: Theoretical and conceptual complexities in the design and analysis of menstrual cycle research, in The Menstrual Cycle, Volume 2: Research and Implications for Women's Health. Edited by Nowack JA, Elder SN. New York, Springer-Verlag, 1981

Kratcoski PC: Child abuse and violence against the family. Child Welfare 61:435–444, 1982

Lewis DO, Shanok SS: Medical histories of delinquent and nondelinquent children. Am J Psychiatry 134:1020–1025, 1977

Lewis DO, Shanok SS, Pincus JH, et al: Violent juvenile delinquents: psychiatric, neurological, psychological and abuse factors. J Am Acad Child Psychiatry 18:307–319, 1979

Lewis DO, Moy E, Jackson LD, et al: Biopsychological characteristics of children who later murder: a prospective study. Am J Psychiatry 142:1161–1167, 1985

Light RJ: Abused and neglected children in America: a study of alternative policies. Harvard Education Review 43:556–598, 1974

Loeber R, Dishion T: Early predictors of male delinquency: a review. Psychol Bull 94:68–99, 1983

Martin HP, Beezley P: Behavioral observations of abused children. Dev Med Child Neurol 19:373–387, 1977

Martin HP, Beezley P, Conway EF, et al: The development of abused children. Adv Pediatr 21:25–73, 1974

McCord J: A forty year perspective on effects of child abuse and neglect. Child Abuse Negl 7:265–270, 1983

Monahan J: Predicting Violent Behavior: An Assessment of Clinical Techniques. Beverly Hills, Calif, Sage Publications, 1981

Monane M, Leichter D, Lewis DO: Physical abuse in psychiatrically hospitalized children and adolescents. J Am Acad Child Psychiatry 23:653–658, 1984

Mouzakitis CM: An inquiry into the problem of child abuse and juvenile delinquency, in Exploring the Relationship Between Child Abuse and Delinquency. Edited by Hunner RJ, Walker PYE. Montclair, NJ, Allanheld, Osmun, 1981, p 220–232

Newberger EH, Reed RB, Daniel JH, et al: Pediatric social illness: toward an etiological classification. Pediatrics 50:178–185, 1977

Newberger EH, Newberger CM, Hampton RL: Child abuse: the current theory base and future research needs. J Am Acad Child Psychiatry 22:262–268, 1983

Pagelow MD: Family Violence. New York, Praeger, 1984

Pelton LH: Child abuse and neglect: the myth of classlessness. Am J Orthopsychiatry 48:608–617, 1978

Reidy TJ: The aggressive characteristics of abused and neglected children. J Clin Psychol 33:1140–1145, 1977

Ressler RK, Burgess AW: The men who murdered. FBI Law Enforcement Bulletin 54:2–6, 1985

Rolston RH: The Effect of Prior Physical Abuse on the Expression of Overt and Fantasy Aggressive Behavior in Children. Dissertation Abstracts International 32:3016-B, 1971

Sears RR, Maccoby EE, Levin H: Patterns of Child Rearing. New York, Harper & Row, 1957

Silver LR, Dublin CC, Lourie RS: Does violence breed violence? Contributions from a study of the child abuse syndrome. Am J Psychiatry 126:152–155, 1969

Smith CP, Berkman DJ, Fraser WM: A Preliminary National Assessment of Child Abuse and Neglect and the Juvenile Justice System: The Shadows of Distress. Reports of the National Juvenile Justice Assessment Centers. Washington, DC, US Department of Justice, Office of Juvenile Justice and Delinquency Prevention, 1979

Sommer B: Stress and menstrual distress. J Human Stress 4:5–47, 1978

Sorrells JM: Kids who kill. Crime and Delinquency 23:312–320, 1977

Spinetta JJ, Rigler D: The child-abusing parent: a psychological review. Psychol Bull 77:296–304, 1972

Straus M, Gelles R, Steinmetz SK: Behind Closed Doors: Violence in the American Family. Garden City, NY, Anchor Press, 1980

Tanay E: Adolescents who kill parents: reactive patricide. Aust NZ J Psychiatry 7:263–277, 1973

Tarter RE, Hegedus AM, Winsten NE, et al: Neuropsychological, personality, and familial characteristics of physically abused delinquents. J Am Acad Child Psychiatry 23:668–674, 1984

Wasserman GA, Green A, Allen R: Going beyond abuse: maladaptive patterns of interaction in abusing mother-infant pairs. J Am Acad Child Psychiatry 22:245–252, 1983

Webster W: Crime in the United States—1977. Federal Bureau of Investigation. Washington, DC, US Government Printing Office, 1978

Wick SC: Child abuse as causation of juvenile delinquency in Central Texas, in Exploring the Relationship Between Child Abuse and Delinquency. Edited by Hunner RJ, Walker PYE. Montclair, NJ, Allanheld, Osmun, 1981, pp 233–239

Yarrow MR, Campbell JD, Burton RV: Recollections of childhood: a study of the retrospective method. Monogr Soc Res Child Dev Vol 35, No 5, 1970

Young L: Wednesday's Child: A Study of Child Neglect and Abuse. New York, McGraw-Hill, 1964

Zalba S: Battered children. Transaction 8:58–61, 1971

Chapter 8

Inpatient Psychiatric Violence: Its Course and Associated Symptomatology

Menahem I. Krakowski, M.D., Ph.D.
Judith Jaeger, Ph.D.
Jan Volavka, M.D., Ph.D.

Chapter 8

Inpatient Psychiatric Violence: Its Course and Associated Symptomatology

A better understanding of the behaviors and symptoms that accompany violence in psychiatric populations would facilitate its prediction and control. Epidemiological data, such as the incidence and prevalence of violence in different diagnostic groups (Evenson et al. 1974; MacDonald 1967; Madden et al. 1976; Tuason 1971), have been primarily emphasized in the literature on psychiatric violence. These data are often contradictory. In addition, as the great majority of patients in any given diagnostic group are not violent, diagnosis per se has little predictive value. A more detailed study of the relationship between psychiatric symptomatology and violent behavior might provide important additional information.

Some authors have shared their clinical observations that there appears to be an association between violence and specific psychiatric symptoms including delusions, hallucinations (Planansky and Johnston 1977), and depression (Bach-y-Rita and Veno 1974; Tardiff and Sweillam 1982). A few systematic studies of the relationship between violence and psychopathology have also been reported. Yesavage and co-workers documented a positive relationship between hallucinations, conceptual disorganization, and unusual thought content on the Brief Psychiatric Rating Scale (BPRS) (Overall and Gorham 1962) and incidence of violence during the week following admission. Interestingly, these symptoms were more strongly predictive of violence than were hostility and paranoia ratings on that same scale (Yesavage 1983a, 1983b; Yesavage et al. 1981). These authors concluded that, in the context of serious psychiatric impairment, violence may occur even when manifest hostility is low.

Aspects of the violent patient's functioning other than psychopathology have virtually been ignored in the literature. Assessment

151

of social adaptation and participation in daily ward activities are very important as they might indicate whether violence is part of a more generalized syndrome of social dysfunction or an isolated phenomenon.

Violence in psychiatric populations fluctuates over time, yet its course has received little attention in the literature. In most studies in which data on incidence are reported, values are summed over time, and longitudinal patterns are not studied. A few studies do indicate a wide range in the course of violence as a function of diagnostic group. In acute psychosis, violence is often transient; it is a more chronic characteristic in certain personality disorders (Kermani 1981; Soloff 1978). Hospitalized patients with diagnoses of personality disorder show fairly constant levels of aggression throughout their stay, in contrast to psychotic patients who show a decrease in aggression over time (Kermani 1981; Soloff 1978). No reports have been published on the course of violent behavior in light of the course of psychopathology and social impairment.

A serious methodological shortcoming in the study of psychiatric violence has been the lack of a reliable method for reporting incidents. Studies conducted in inpatient facilities have relied almost exclusively on retrospective examination of incident reports. These often underestimate the incidence of violence (Lion et al. 1981) and are poorly standardized. Careful assessments of assaultive behavior have been rare (Yudofsky et al. 1986).

We designed the present study to correct some of these shortcomings. We examined the associations among violence, level of psychiatric symptomatology, and social functioning on a longitudinal basis in a sample of violent psychiatric inpatients. In addition to the cross-sectional correlations of these variables, we were interested in describing their relative courses and how they varied as a function of diagnosis and age of onset of illness.

SUBJECTS AND METHODS

All of the subjects studied were inpatients at Manhattan Psychiatric Center. This is a 1,300-bed psychiatric hospital located in New York City and serving predominantly indigent inner-city patients. Subjects in the present study were 44 consecutive admissions to a special 15-bed unit designed for the management and study of violent inpatient behavior. Patients were never admitted directly to this special ward from the community; they had to exhibit at least two instances of assaultive behavior directed at others on their "home" wards in order to be transferred to the special ward.

The diagnosis of all patients was established by a consensus of two research psychiatrists using DSM-III (American Psychiatric Association 1980) criteria. The diagnostic distribution of our sample was as follows: schizophrenia, 25 patients; major affective disorder, 6; personality disorder, 6; and mental retardation, 7. The mean (± SD) age of the 14 female and 30 male patients was 31.1 ± 9.1. The mean age at first psychiatric hospitalization was 16.4 ± 6.20, and patients had been ill for a mean of 14.8 ± 8.0 years. The mean length of stay on the special unit for the current admission was 51.6 ± 25.9 days. Patients were discharged from the unit when their behavior was stabilized. The study was conducted over a period of approximately 8 months.

Violence Data

Special emphasis was placed in this study on careful monitoring of all violent incidents and not just those reported in nurses' incident reports. The unit had a staff-to-patient ratio of approximately 1-to-1 during daytime hours, and 1-to-2 for evening hours. Since patients were restricted to a large dayroom most of the time, constant observation of patient behavior was possible.

The investigators assessed and categorized ward violence by means of direct on-site observations or by telephone or personal interviews with staff at the end of each shift. This was done on a 24-hour basis. Data analyzed for a 4-month period revealed that more than twice the number of incidents were detected using this method than through nurses' reports.

All aggressive incidents were rated using the Scale for the Assessment of Aggressive and Agitated Behaviors (Brizer et al. 1987). Incidents were recorded and characterized as falling into one of four categories: physical assault against others (which included any physically aggressive act directed against another individual), verbal assault (which consisted of a verbal threat of bodily harm directed at an individual), assault against property (such as throwing objects), and agitation (which included nonfocused shouting or markedly increased psychomotor activity). We included agitation in our study because we had observed that in our population of chronically violent patients, agitation often escalated to more severe forms of violence when not controlled by staff intervention. Preliminary results also indicated a positive correlation between agitation and assault against property (Pearson r = .59, 42 df, p < .01). Both agitation and assault against property were considered to be undirected or unfocused acts of aggression, whereas assault against others and verbal assault were considered to be directed or focused acts of aggression. Kappa coefficients for interrater reliability in categorizing the four types of violence was above .95 ($p < .01$).

Psychiatric Symptomatology

Two raters evaluated the patients using the BPRS. One rated the patients weekly and the other intermittently. Interrator reliability was established at the outset of the study and intermittently reevaluated. Pearson rs remained above .93 throughout the study. In addition to the total BPRS score, we examined two of the five factors reported by Overall and Gorham. Factor 3, "thought disturbance," includes the following items of the BPRS: conceptual disorganization, hallucinatory behavior, and unusual thought content. Factor 5, "hostile-suspiciousness," includes hostility, suspiciousness, uncooperativeness, and grandiosity.

Evaluation of Social Dysfunction

Each patient's level of social adaptation on the ward was assessed by the ward's activity therapists who interact with the patients closely on a daily basis. An assessment was made of each patient's behavior as he participated in four major activities with the therapist: daily exercise, grooming, social interaction (during group discussions), and recreational activities. Each of these four areas was rated on a 5-point scale, with increasing score indicating increasing dysfunction. Two raters (activity therapists) provided the weekly ratings for a period of 8 weeks. The Pearson r correlation for interrater reliability was .85 ($p < .01$). For the remaining time, a single rater provided data.

Data Analysis

The weekly frequencies of violent events and their subtypes were recorded throughout each patient's stay. For the purpose of this report, 3 target weeks were selected for data analysis: the first, middle, and last weeks of each patient's stay on the ward. All tests used were two-tailed.

Pearson r correlations were used to examine the relationship between violence and the clinical measures (BPRS and social dysfunction) cross-sectionally at each of the three time periods for the total group of 44 patients and separately for the more homogeneous subset of 31 patients with schizophrenia or major affective disorder, called the functional disorder group. Correlation coefficients were also computed between percentage of change in violence and percentage of change in each of the clinical variables over the time intervals first till middle week and middle week till last week.

Group comparisons were made between the 31 patients with functional disorders and the 13 with either personality disorder or mental retardation at the 3 target weeks using repeated-measures analysis of variance (ANOVA). Pearson correlations were used to assess how age at first hospitalization was related to violence and to the clinical variables.

RESULTS

Violence and Its Clinical Correlates

In the total group of subjects, BPRS and social dysfunction scores showed a pattern of positive and significant correlations with frequency of assault against property and agitation (unfocused violence) but not with frequency of verbal or physical assaults against others (focused violence) (see Table 1).

When these correlations were repeated for the 31 patients with functional disorders alone, no significant correlations between total BPRS scores and violence emerged at any of the 3 target weeks. Social dysfunction, however, correlated positively and significantly with the total number of violent incidents during the first week

Table 1. Frequencies of unfocused violence correlated with BPRS and social dysfunction scores

Clinical variables	Assault against property		Agitation	
	r	df	r	df
First week				
BPRS	.32*	39	ns	
Social dysfunction	ns		ns	
Middle week				
BPRS	.30*	43	.27(*)	43
Social dysfunction	.38*	36	.39*	36
Last week				
BPRS	.40**	40	ns	
Social dysfunction	.35*	38	ns	

Note. (*)$p < .10$; *$p < .05$; **$p < .01$; ns = not significant

($r = .41$, 22 df, $p < .05$) and with verbal assault during the middle week ($r = .44$, 24 df, $p < .05$).

Among the individual BPRS factors, we found consistent negative associations between the hostile-suspiciousness factor and measures of violence. In the patients with functional disorders, the correlation with assault against property in the middle week of stay was significant ($r = -.35$, 30 df, $p < .05$). Similar trends emerged for this factor in the total sample: there was a negative correlation with assault against others for the first week of stay ($r = -.29$, 38 df, $p < .10$) and with verbal assault for the last week of stay ($r = -.29$, 39 df, $p < .10$).

Reduction in Violence and Its Clinical Correlates

Subjects showed significant reduction in the total number of violent incidents during their stay on the unit, seen by comparing number of incidents during the first week of their stay to number of incidents during the last week ($t = 2.26$, 39 df, $p < .05$).

The percentage of change in the total number of violent incidents over the first and second halves of the patients' stays on the unit was correlated with the corresponding changes in clinical variables. Percentage of improvement in total BPRS, thought disturbance factor, and social dysfunction scores correlated significantly with reduction of violence during the first half of stay. In the second half, only improvement in social functioning was significantly correlated with reduction in violence (see Table 2).

Diagnostic Groups

Repeated measures ANOVA comparing patients with functional disorders and those without (the personality disorder or mental retardation group) on the violence variables as a function of time revealed several group main effects. Total violence ($F = 9.24$, 37/1 df, $p < .01$) and assault against property ($F = 6.77$, 37/1 df, $p < .05$) were significantly different in the two groups, with patients with personality disorder or mental retardation being more violent than those with functional disorders. There was a trend in the same direction for physical ($F = 3.88$, 37/1 df, $p < .10$) and verbal assaults ($F = 3.50$, 37/1 df, $p < .10$). There was a significant group × week interaction for verbal assaults ($F = 4.67$, 37/1 df, $p < .05$), indicating that the patients with functional disorders were initially more verbally abusive than those without functional disorders but became less so during their stay, whereas the reverse was true of the patients with personality disorder or mental retardation (see Figure 1.)

Age at First Hospitalization

Age at first hospitalization was significantly and negatively correlated with violent incidents during the middle ($r = -.50$, 42 df, $p < .01$) and last week of stay ($r = -.39$, 42 df, $p < .01$) and with the total BPRS score during the last week of stay ($r = .-36$, 40 df, $p <. 05$) and middle week of stay ($r = -.27$, 42 df, $p <. 10$). The younger the patient was at first hospitalization, the more likely he was to show persistence of violence and psychopathology later in his stay on the unit despite treatment. When the change in psychopathology (BPRS score) from first to last week was considered, the younger the patient was at first hospitalization, the less the change in psychopathology during his stay on the unit ($r = .45$, 35 df, $p < .01$). Similar results were obtained for the restricted sample of patients with functional disorders.

DISCUSSION

Violence in psychiatric patients can be better understood when it is studied in a broader behavioral context. It emerges, then, as a more differentiated phenomenon. A dissociation between focused violence (verbal assaults and assaults against others) and unfocused violence

Table 2. Percentage change in violence correlated with percentage change in BPRS, BPRS factors, and social dysfunction for the two time intervals

	r	df
Changes in scores over the first time interval (first to middle week)		
BPRS total score	.40**	38
Thought disturbance factor	.47**	37
Hostile-suspiciousness factor	ns	
Social dysfunction score	.44**	32
Changes in scores over the second time interval (middle to last week)		
BPRS total score	ns	
Thought disturbance factor	ns	
Hostile-suspiciousness factor	ns	
Social dysfunction score	.33*	35

Note. *$p < .05$; **$p < .01$; ns = not significant.

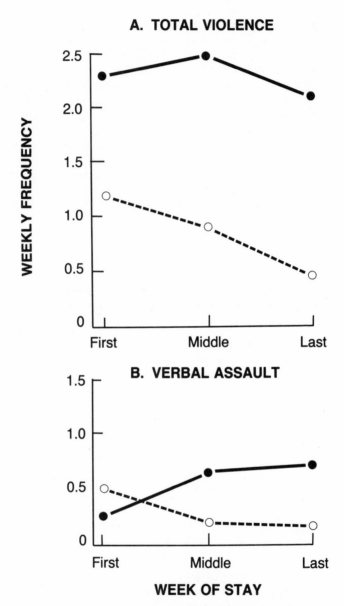

Figure 1. Comparisons of 31 patients with functional disorders (solid line) and 13 patients with personality disorder or mental retardation (broken line) on total violence and verbal assault

(assaults against property and agitation) emerged. It is the latter that is closely associated with a high level of psychiatric disturbance and social dysfunction. A more disorganized state expresses itself in haphazard violence.

Violence showed a more consistent association with social dysfunction than with psychiatric symptomatology. It would thus appear to be more indicative of a general disruption of social functioning than of intrapsychic disturbances. The fact that a patient is functioning poorly during ward activities may be a more important danger signal than his being psychotic. This is of considerable practical value because social functioning, as assessed here, was based purely on behavioral observations. Its assessment does not require patients' cooperation or extensive raters' training, in contrast to psychiatric symptomatology scales, such as the BPRS.

Improvement in social functioning was consistently paralleled by a decrease in violence throughout the patients' stay on the unit. A decrease in psychiatric symptomatology, on the other hand, was accompanied by a decrease in violence only during the first half of stay, not the second. Psychiatric symptomatology may be, in part, responsible for the emergence of violence in psychiatric patients in the more acute phase of illness. There can be a further decrease in violence and an improvement in social functioning despite the persistence of some psychiatric symptoms.

Paranoia and hostility, which are often assumed to be conducive to assaultive behavior, did not, in fact, show a positive association with violence. Percentage of change in violence correlated positively with percentage of change in social dysfunction, total BPRS score, and thought disturbance, but not with paranoia and hostility. These results support the findings by Yesavage (1983a, 1983b) and Yesavage et al. (1981) noted above. As all patients had to be violent to be admitted to the study sample, this finding may indicate that after an initial violent outburst, paranoid patients tend to be especially cautious to avoid further conflict. This is consistent with reports in the literature that paranoid patients are most often violent prior to admission, but rarely so after some time in treatment (Planansky and Johnston 1977; Shader et al. 1977; Tardiff and Sweillam 1980, 1982; Yesavage 1983a, 1983b).

Violence was investigated here as a behavior that is variable over time. The frequency of violent incidents tended to decrease over time. In some patients, however, violence and psychiatric symptomatology persisted despite treatment. These patients' may have a different type of illness as indicated by a younger age of onset. The younger the patients were when first hospitalized, the more likely they were to show continuous psychopathology and violence in the latter part of their stay on the unit.

There is also some indication that violence varies in different diagnostic groups. The patients with a diagnosis of personality disorder or mental retardation were considerably more violent than the patients with a diagnosis of schizophrenia or major affective disorder. Furthermore, their violence showed less response to treatment.

REFERENCES

American Psychiatric Association: Diagnostic and Statistical Manual of Mental Disorders, 3rd ed (DSM-III). Washington, DC, American Psychiatric Association, 1980

Bach-y-Rita G, Veno A: Habitual violence: a profile of 62 men. Am J Psychiatry 131:1015–1017, 1974

Brizer DB, Convit A, Krakowski M, et al: A rating scale for reporting violence on psychiatric wards. Hosp Community Psychiatry 38:769–770, 1987

Evenson RC, Altman H, Sletten IW, et al: Disturbing behavior: a study of incident reports. Psychiatr Q 48:266–275, 1974

Kermani EJ: Violent psychiatric patients: a study. Am J Psychother 35:215–225, 1981

Lion R, Snyder W, Merrill G: Underreporting of assaults on staff in a state hospital. Hosp Community Psychiatry 32:497–498, 1981

MacDonald JM: Homicidal threats. Am J Psychiatry 124:475–482, 1967

Madden DJ, Lion LR, Penna MW: Assault on psychiatrists by patients. Am J Psychiatry 133:422–425, 1976

Overall JE, Gorham DR: The Brief Psychiatric Rating Scale. Psychol Reports 10:799–812, 1962

Planansky K, Johnston R: Homicidal aggression in schizophrenic men. Acta Psychiatr Scand 55:65–73, 1977

Shader RI, Jackson AH, Harmatz JS, et al: Patterns of violent behavior among schizophrenic inpatients. Diseases of the Nervous System 38:13–16, 1977

Soloff PH: Behavioral precipitants of restraints in the modern milieu. Compr Psychiatry 19:179–184, 1978

Tardiff K, Sweillam A: Assault, suicide and mental illness. Arch Gen Psychiatry 37:164–169, 1980

Tardiff K, Sweillam A: Assaultive behavior among chronic inpatients. Am J Psychiatry 139:212–215, 1982

Tuason VB: The psychiatrist and the violent patient. Diseases of the Nervous System 32:764–768, 1971

Yesavage JA: Bipolar illness: correlates of dangerous inpatient behavior. Br J Psychiatry 143:554–557, 1983a

Yesavage JA: Inpatient violence and the schizophrenic patient. Acta Psychiatr Scand 67:353–357, 1983b

Yesavage JA, Werner PD, Becker JM, et al: Inpatient evaluation of aggression in psychiatric patients. J Nerv Ment Dis 169:299–301, 1981

Yudofsky S, Silver J, Jackson W, et al: The overt aggression scale for the objective rating of verbal and physical aggression. Am J Psychiatry 143:35–39, 1986

Chapter 9

Schizophrenic Violence and Psychopathology

Menahem I. Krakowski, M.D., Ph.D.
Jan Volavka, M.D., Ph.D.

Chapter 9

Schizophrenic Violence and Psychopathology

Schizophrenics figure prominently among violent psychiatric patients. To be able to predict and control violence in this group, various aspects of the disease, such as schizophrenic symptomatology, course of illness, and subtype of schizophrenia, must be investigated in relation to violence.

PSYCHIATRIC DIAGNOSIS AND VIOLENCE

Is violence more common in schizophrenia than in other psychiatric disorders? Many studies have compared the incidence of violence in different diagnostic groups. Patients with a broad range of violent behaviors have been studied in a variety of settings. There is, therefore, a great deal of heterogeneity in the demographic and psychiatric characteristics of the patient samples studied.

There are special methodological problems with regard to diagnosis and selection of subject populations when we deal with violent patients. The violence itself may influence both the diagnosis and the disposition of the patient, which creates selective bias. The diagnosis of psychotic individuals with mild illness may be disproportionately influenced by the presence of deviant violent behavior when it is the predominant clinical feature. Thus schizophrenic patients can be misdiagnosed as antisocial personalities (Travin and Protter 1982). Violence can be associated with the onset of schizophrenia in adolescents; in such cases it is even more likely to be dismissed by being categorized under a label of "conduct disorder" or "unsocialized aggressive reaction" (Inamder et al. 1982).

When the illness is more obvious, the tendency is to view the aggressive behavior as part of the illness. These patients are more likely to be correctly diagnosed as having schizophrenia or some other psychotic disorder. They are also more likely to be hospitalized than arrested or referred to outpatient treatment. In a study of persons presented by the police for civil commitment, less than half of individuals seen as potentially dangerous to others were considered for arrest (Monahan et al. 1979). Violent patients were also more likely to be hospitalized than referred for outpatient treatment or crisis intervention if they were psychotic, and especially if they were schizophrenic (Skodol and Karasu 1980). Selective bias can occur because certain institutions will make an effort to exclude patients with a history of violent attacks on people (Karson and Bigelow 1987).

Given these methodological limitations, it is surprising to see how consistently schizophrenia is associated with a high incidence of violence in the literature (Craig 1982; Karson and Bigelow 1987; Pearson et al. 1983; Shader et al. 1977; Sosowsky 1978; Tardiff and Sweillam 1980, 1982; Zitrin et al. 1976). Violence is reported in a variety of different settings, with a wide range in the type of behavior labeled violent: these range from verbal threats or haphazard striking to well-planned murders. With other diagnoses, violence is usually restricted to a specific setting and type. For example, organic mental syndrome has been associated with high inpatient violence and unfocused assaults (Petrie et al. 1982), but not with a high arrest rate for violent crime.

The literature is much less consistent as to what percentage of schizophrenics are violent. Estimates ranged from as low as 8 percent (Fottrell 1980) to as high as 45 percent of patients with schizophrenia (Karson and Bigelow 1987; Shader et al. 1977). Selective biases mentioned above are clearly operant here. Of special importance here is how broad a definition of violence is used and what period of time is surveyed. Cultural factors and a diagnostic bias also appear to play an important role; European studies usually report a lower incidence of violence than American ones.

Although diagnosis is an important variable in the prediction of violence, it is not in and of itself sufficient to afford accurate prediction. Many other aspects of schizophrenia must be explored to see their connection to violence.

COURSE OF ILLNESS AND VIOLENCE

When is violence most likely to appear in the course of the illness? In one study of 74 schizophrenics referred because of acts of violence, only 37 percent of these acts had taken place during a psychotic episode (Virkkunen 1974). Most studies, however, have found that schizophrenia is most likely to be associated with an increased risk of assaultive behavior during the acute psychotic episode. Frequency of violent incidents tends to reflect the course of psychosis and to be positively related to the severity of psychotic symptoms.

In one study of 205 hospitalized schizophrenics (Planansky and Johnston 1977), overt expressions of aggression, whether verbal or physical, occurred most frequently during acute episodes and especially in the first episode of the illness (as opposed to subsequent episodes). In another study of inpatients with various diagnoses but where most of the violent acts had been committed by schizophrenics, significantly more assaults occurred in the first 10 days subsequent to admission than at other times during hospitalization (Rofman et al. 1980).

SCHIZOPHRENIC SYMPTOMATOLOGY AND VIOLENT BEHAVIOR

One study (Virkkunen 1974) reported that the majority of schizophrenics were not actively psychotic when they committed violent acts. Violence in these patients is seen as resulting more frequently from interpersonal difficulties than from psychotic symptoms. Longstanding hostility and resentment toward the victim culminated in an act of violence (Virkkunen 1984). Most studies, however, report the presence of psychotic symptomatology at the time of violence. The association between these symptoms and violence has been investigated in different ways. Often an attempt has been made to explain the psychopathology of and motivation for the violent act once it has been committed. Several studies report that violence was accompanied by hallucinations and delusions (Hafner and Boker 1973; Lanzkron 1963; Planansky and Johnston 1977; Reichard and Tilman 1950; Taylor 1985).

In Planansky and Johnston's (1977) report, violence in 59 schizophrenic men was accompanied by severe hallucinations and delusions. The most common presentation for these patients was gross delusional, hallucinatory disorganization with prominent psychotic fears and loss of control. There were also six patients with illnesses of "catatonic types" in whom violence was characterized by unprovoked destruction of property and self-injury, in addition to explosive, murderous attacks.

In some studies, delusions were more commonly found in association with violence than were hallucinations. Hafner and Boker (1973) reported on systematized delusions about spouses or significant others, with acts of violence often directed at these people. Another study (Taylor 1985) reported that out of 121 violent psychotic male prisoners (of whom the majority were schizophrenic), all but 9 showed active symptoms at the time of committing a criminal offense. Delusions were common. Those driven to offend by their delusions were more likely to have been seriously violent. In the latter two studies the schizophrenics were not classified according to sub-type. It is possible that some of the patients with prominent delusions would have been classified as paranoid schizophrenics. The presentation of violence (its severity and its occurrence in the context of interpersonal tensions) is consistent with the one described in paranoid schizophrenia (see section below).

Yesavage (Chapter 4) approached the issue of psychopathology and violence from a different perspective. He correlated severity of symptomatology in acutely psychotic schizophrenics with subsequent violent behavior. Symptomatology was assessed by the Brief Psychiatric Rating Scale (BPRS). Scores on the BPRS items indicating conceptual disorganization, hallucinations, and unusual thought content showed positive correlations with the rate of violence in the week following admission. BPRS subscales that related to paranoid symptoms were also significantly correlated, but to a somewhat lesser degree.

SUBTYPES OF SCHIZOPHRENIA

Several studies have analyzed the occurrence of violence in different subtypes of schizophrenia. Most of these have divided schizophrenic patients into two groups: paranoid and nonparanoid. The latter group is variable in composition, including in one study a high percentage of schizoaffective patients (Shader et al. 1977) and in another almost entirely chronic undifferentiated schizophrenics (Addad et al. 1981). There are also variations in chronicity between the two groups. In one study the paranoid schizophrenics were the patients with the more chronic illness (Blackburn 1968). The use of admission diagnoses (which are notoriously unreliable) probably increased the percentage of patients diagnosed as paranoid schizophrenics in one study (Planansky and Johnston 1977). Of eight studies comparing the incidence of violence in these two groups, five found paranoid schizophrenics to be more violent than nonparanoid schizophrenics (Addad et al. 1981; Blackburn 1968; Planansky and Johnston 1977; Rossi et al. 1986; Tardiff and Sweillam 1980), two studies reported the nonparanoid group as more violent (Shader et al. 1977; Tardiff and Sweillam 1982), and one study found no differences between these two subtypes (Yesavage 1983). While it is possible that some of the methodological inconsistencies described above contributed to these conflicting results, it is interesting to note that they may be explained on the basis of the difference in times at which assessment was made.

Studies reporting a greater incidence of violence in paranoid patients assessed violence prior to admission or throughout the active phase of the illness. Studies reporting more violence in nonparanoid patients, on the other hand, focused on inpatients who had been in the hospital for a considerable period of time. The study that found no difference in violence between these two groups investigated its occurrence at an intermediate time between these two extremes. The variation in prevalence of violence may reflect the different course and response to treatment in the various subtypes: paranoid schizophrenics do evidence more violence than other schizophrenics, but respond to treatment more quickly and remit more thoroughly once they are in a hospital setting. Nonparanoid patients remain more symptomatic and more assaultive.

Several studies have focused on qualitative differences in the violence of paranoid and nonparanoid schizophrenics. When severity of violence is considered, it is found that paranoid schizophrenics are consistently overrepresented among the seriously violent patients. In one study, assault was rated in four categories according to severity (Rofman et al. 1980). Significantly more patients with paranoid schizophrenia than with any other diagnosis or subtype of schizophrenia committed assaults of the most severe form. Murder, the most extreme type of physical assault, is particularly frequent among paranoid schizophrenics (Lunde 1975; McKnight et al. 1966).

More extensive descriptions of the violent act and the context in which it occurs have been provided in the literature. In one study by Benezech et al. (1980) conducted at a French hospital for the criminally insane, the greatest frequency of violent crimes against persons was found in the paranoid group. These patients had fixed and well-developed delusions, on which they acted. This often led to serious aggressive acts that were frequently directed at family members. In another study, conducted in several French mental institutions and focusing on schizophrenics only, these investigators (Addad et al. 1981) contrasted the paranoid schizophrenics to the chronic undifferentiated schizophrenics. The paranoid schizophrenics were more likely to commit a crime against persons and to act against family and friends; they were more likely to cite vengeance as their motivation for the crime. In contrast, the chronic undifferentiated schizophrenics cited profit as their main motivation.

This same characterization of the paranoid group can also be seen in geriatric patient populations: the paraphrenic patients with systemized paranoid delusions are more likely to be dangerous than other violent geriatric patients. They tend to act in line with their delusions to defend themselves against their "persecutors." They are much more likely to plan their attack and to have recourse to weapons.

CONCLUSION

These studies are consistent in the description they provide of these two contrasting forms of violence. In the paranoid subtype, some form of delusion is prominent, and the violence that ensues is usually well planned and in line with the delusion. The interpersonal element is of great importance: the violence is directed at a specific person, usually a significant individual in the patient's life, who is seen as prescribing or depriving the patient of some basic need. In contrast, the violence occurring in the other subtypes of schizophrenia is less focused, less planned, and often less dangerous.

REFERENCES

Addad M, Benezech M, Bourgeois M, et al: Criminal acts among schizophrenics in French mental hospitals. J Nerv Ment Dis 169:289–293, 1981

Benezech M, Bourgeois M, Yesavage J: Violence in the mentally ill: a study of 547 patients at a French hospital for the criminally insane. J Nerv Ment Dis 168:698–700, 1980

Blackburn R: Emotionality, extraversion, and aggression of paranoid and nonparanoid schizophrenic offenders. Br J Psychiatry 115:1301–1302, 1968

Craig TJ: An epidemiologic study of problems associated with violence among psychiatric inpatients. Am J Psychiatry 139:1262–1266, 1982

Fottrell E: A study of violent behavior among patients in psychiatric hospitals. Br J Psychiatry 136:216–221, 1980

Hafner H. Boker W: Mentally disordered violent offenders. Soc Psychiatry 8:220–229, 1973

Inamdar S, Lewis D, Siaomopoulos G, et al: Violent and suicidal behavior in psychotic adolescents. Am J Psychiatry 139:932–935, 1982

Karson C, Bigelow LB: Violent behavior in schizophrenic patients. J Nerv Ment Dis 175:161–164, 1987

Lanzkron J: Murder and insanity: a survey. Am J Psychiatry 119:754–758, 1963

Lunde DT: Murder and Madness. Stanford, The Stanford Alumni Association, the Portable Stanford, 1975

McKnight CK, Mohr JW, Quincey RE, et al: Mental illness and homicide. Canadian Psychiatric Association Journal 11:91–98, 1966

Monahan J, Caldeira C, Friedlander H: Police and the mentally ill. Int J Law Psychiatry 2:508–518, 1979

Pearson M, Wilmot E, Padi M: A study of violent behavior among inpatients in psychiatric hospitals. Br J Psychiatry 149:232–234, 1986

Petrie WM, Lawson EC, Hollender MH: Violence in geriatric patients. JAMA 248:443–444, 1982

Plananski K, Johnston R: Homicidal aggression in schizophrenic men. Acta Psychiatr Scand 55:65–73, 1977

Reichard S, Tillman C: Murder and suicide as defenses against scizophrenic psychosis. J Clin Psychopath 11:149–163, 1950

Rofman ES, Askinazi C, Fant C: The prediction of dangerous behavior in emergency civil commitment. Am J Psychiatry 137:1061–1064, 1980

Rossi AM, Jacobs M, Monteleone M, et al: Characteristics of psychiatric patients who engage in assaultive or other fear-inducing behaviors. J Nerv Ment Dis 174:154–160, 1986

Shader RI, Jackson AH, Harmatz JS, et al: Patterns of violent behavior among schizophrenic inpatients. Diseases of the Nervous System 38:13–16, 1977

Skodol AE, Karasu TB: Toward hospitalization criteria for violent patients. Compr Psychiatry 21:162–166, 1980

Sosowsky L: Crime and violence among mental patients reconsidered in view of the new legal relationships between the state and the mentally ill. Am J Psychiatry 37:33–42, 1978

Tardiff K, Sweillam A: Assault, suicide and mental illness. Arch Gen Psychiatry 37:164–169, 1980

Tardiff K, Sweillam A: Assaultive behavior among chronic inpatients. Am J Psychiatry 139:212–215, 1982

Taylor T: Motives for offending among violent and psychotic men. Br J Psychiatry 147:491–498, 1985

Travin S, Protler B: Mad or Bad? Some clinical considerations in the misdiagnosis of schizophrenia as antisocial personality disorder. Am J Psychiatry 139:1335–1338, 1982

Virkkunen M: Observations of violence in schizophrenia. Acta Psychiatr Scand 50:145–151, 1974

Yesavage JA: Inpatient violence and the schizophrenic patient. Acta Psychiatr Scand 67:353–357, 1983

Zitrin A, Hardesty AS, Burdock EU, et al: Crime and violence among mental patients. Am J Psychiatry 133:142–149, 1976